텝스의 기술

텝스의 기술

초판 1쇄 발행일 2014년 1월 27일
초판 4쇄 발행일 2016년 9월 12일

지은이 송승호
펴낸이 양옥매
디자인 오현숙
표지디자인 박무선

펴낸곳 도서출판 책과나무
출판등록 제2012-000376
주소 서울특별시 마포구 방울내로 79 이노빌딩 302호
대표전화 02.372.1537 **팩스** 02.372.1538
이메일 booknamu2007@naver.com
홈페이지 www.booknamu.com
ISBN 978-89-98528-96-6(13740)

이 도서의 국립중앙도서관 출판시도서목록(CIP)은 서지정보유통지원 시스템
홈페이지(http://seoji.nl.go.kr)와 국가자료공동목록시스템
(http://www.nl.go.kr/kolisnet)에서 이용하실 수 있습니다.
(CIP제어번호 : CIP2014001959)

텝스의 기술

송승호 외 18명 저

'단순 요령' 이 아닌, 원리 원칙 대로 풀어나가는 전략
서울 강남 대치 지역 전석 매진 기적의 강의

www.teps19.com

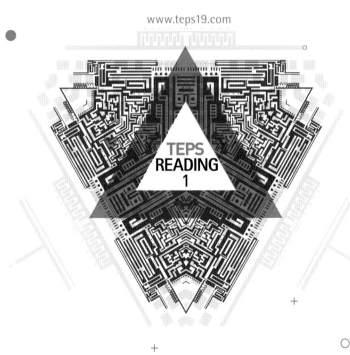

TEPS
READING
1

책과나무

Content

I. 전체전략

II. 지문공략법

BASIC

INTERMEDIATE

ADVANCED

Ⅲ. 선택지공략법

Ⅳ. 체화과정

독해 2편

Ⅰ. 텝스 시험의 전반적인 전략
– 파트 별 팁
– 시험장 실전 전략

Ⅱ. 일치 찾기 유형
– 자체 변화
– 선택지 쏘아보기
– 2가지 유형
– 유형별 문제 풀이 루틴
– 디바이드 기술 및 활용

Ⅲ. 추론 유형
– 유형 설명
– 주제st
– 코렉트st
– 변형 문제

Ⅳ. 파트3 유형
– 쉬운 유형
– 어려운 유형

Ⅴ. 연결어 유형
– (300점 이하) 문제 풀이 루틴
– (300점 이상) 문제 풀이 루틴

Author's Note

저는 텝스 때문에 3년을 고생했습니다.

생애 첫 텝스 시험을 보던 날 정신없이 몰아치는 문제들과 시간적 압박 속에 당황하여 "도대체 이건 뭐 하는 시험이지?" 라고 생각했던 기억이 납니다. 그리고 집에 돌아가서 텝스와 관련된 전략을 찾기 위해 인터넷을 엄청나게 뒤졌지만, 도움되는 내용은 찾을 수가 없었습니다.

그래서 텝스 시험에 적합한 전략을 세우기 위해 스스로 시험을 분석하기 시작했습니다. 텝스와 관련된 모든 전략, 점수대별 공부 방법부터 문제풀이 전략, 문제풀이 기술, 독해 문제 풀이 루틴, 오답을 확실히 발견해내는 기술 등과 같은 텝스 점수 향상에 필요한 모든 전략을 세웠습니다.

그 결과, 수많은 시행착오와 고생 끝에 이론이 완성되었고, 회차 전국 11등을 한 이후로 주위 사람들에게 이 이론을 전달하면서 "텝스19"라는 이름을 붙이게 되었으며, 그들의 성적 또한 빠르게 상승하는 것을 보며 이 콘텐츠는 점수대와 상관없이 모두에게 적용된다는 확신이 생겼습니다.

텝스19 라는 어학원을 2012년 말에 설립한 이후로 1,000명 이상의 학생들이 저에게 직접 텝스의 기술들을 전달 받아, 이 중 상당수가 최단기 점수 향상을 체험하였습니다. 텝스19는 94%의 완강률과 91% 수업 만족도를 자랑하는 만큼 업계 그 어떤 어학원과는 차별화된 퀄리티 높은 콘텐츠를 자랑합니다.

또, [텝스의 기술]은 단순 요령이나 꼼수가 아닙니다.

[텝스의 기술]은 텝스 점수를 1. 최단기간에 2. 최대 점수 폭으로 3. 성적을 극대화시키기 위한 텝스의 모든 전략입니다.

그리고, 마지막으로 텝스에 대한 한 가지 오해를 꼭 풀고 싶은데, 텝스 준비생들 사이에서 "텝스는 기술이 안 통하는 시험" 이라는 속설이 있습 니다.

텝스에 기술이 안 통한다는 것은 그저 소문일 뿐이고, 저를 포함한 수많은 수강생들의 성적이 이를 반증하였습니다.

제가 알기론, 텝스 시험이 원하는 정확한 정답의 기준을 제대로 파악하고 따로 이 부분을 강의하는 사람은 없습니다. [텝스의 기술 독해1편]에서 처음으로 그 부분을 명확하게 다룹니다.

이 책과 강의 내용(www.teps19.com)이 텝스 수험생들에게 올바른 접근법과 시험에 대한 이해도를 확립해 줄 수 있을 것이라고 자신합니다.

[텝스의 기술] 모든 독자들의 성적 상승 기적을 기원하겠습니다. 파이팅 !!

2013년 12월 25일
크리스마스 당일까지 텝스19와 함께하는
송승호 드림.

동영상 강의, 문제분석 강의
www.teps19.com 참고.

STRATEGIC
TEPS

I 전체전략

텝스가
원하는
정답의
기준

0 텝스가 원하는 정답의 기준

텝스 시험에는 정확한 정답의 기준이 존재한다. 어디에서도 이러한 기준을 설명해주지 않지만, 텝스가 원하는 정답의 기준은 분명히 존재한다.

수험생들은 이러한 기준이 정립되지 않았기 때문에 시험을 치를 때 선택지 두 개 사이에서 계속 고민하게 되고, 정답을 바라보면서도 자기 나름대로 다른 오답도 말이 될 수 있지 않을까 하고 합리화 하게 된다.

실제 시험에서도 선택지 두 개 사이에서 고민하다가 한 문제에서 3~4분을 날린 경험이 있을 것이다. 그리고 후회속에 퇴실하며, "다음부턴 그러지 말아야지" 정도의 다짐만으로 반성을 마친다.

하지만 이런 습관은 마음가짐의 변화 정도로 바뀔 수 있는 부분이 아니다. 분명한 기준이 정립 되어야 하며 그 기준이 정립되지 못한다면 다음 시험에서 또다시 선택지 두 개 사이에서 계속 고민하게 될 것이다.그래서 이 책의 모든 단원을 학습하면서도 항상 [0단원] "텝스가 원하는 정답의 기준"의 내용을 생각하며 문제 풀이에 임해야 한다. [0단원]과 [19단원]의 내용만 확실히 체화하면 선택지 두 개 중에 고민하며 허비하는 시간이 줄어들 것이고, 지문을 읽어내는 관점요령도 키울 수 있을 것이다.

정답의 기준이 없는 사람이 쉽게 빠져 들 수 있는 함정들은 너무 많다.

이것은 영어 실력과 무관하여 쉬운 문제들에도 나타난다.

아래 문제를 풀어보도록 하자.

Do you hate having to choose what to wear every day? Would you rather prefer 5 more minutes of sleep than having to decide in the morning what to wear? Then just call ClothesFit today for a 7-day free trial of preselected clothes every morning. We offer competitive monthly expenses, discounts for high school students, and trustworthy courteous service. Sign a monthly contract with us before January 6th and get 19% off. Don't _____ - just call ClothesFit at 466-0542!

(a) lose 5 minutes of your sleep
(b) give your clothes selection another thought
(c) hesitate any longer
(d) worry about the trendiness of the style selection

While the so-called "dumb" phones are disappearing quickly, some other electronic gadgets are disappearing even faster. Digital cameras, portable gaming console, PDAs and mp3 players have almost disappeared off the market since 2010, and they may become completely obsolete by the next few years. The leading factor contributing to their demise is the sheer multi-functionality of smart phones. With their phones becoming more versatile and compact than ever, people are no longer feeling the need for bulky separate devices.

Q. What is the passage mainly about?
(a) The inconvenience of using separate devices
(b) The demise of numerous electronic devices.
(c) The disappearance of dumb phones from the market
(d) The versatility and compactness of smartphones

다 풀 때까지 페이지를 넘기지 말자.
정답은 다음 페이지에.

1번 문제는

아마 A, B, C 중에 고민을 했을 것이다.

그렇다면 정답은 무엇일까? 그리고 정답은 하나뿐일까?

정답은 B다.

A와 C는 정답이 될 수 없는 이유가 명확히 존재한다.

(이 문제에 대한 정답의 기준은 [7단원]에서 확인하도록 하자)

이 문제를 만약 시험장에서 접했다면 여러분의 대다수는 이 문제에 2분 이상의 시간을 투자하였을 것이다.

왜냐? 지문 자체가 쉬우므로 '이렇게 쉬운 문제를 틀리면 아깝다'는 생각이 들기 때문이다. 하지만 정답의 기준이 없기 때문에 결국 고민 끝에 A, B, C 중에 하나를 찍게 되는 것이다.

정답의 기준만 확실하다면 30초 안에도 풀 수 있었던 문제인데 말이다.

2번 문제는 정답이 B일까 D일까?

정답은 B다. 이것도 마찬가지로 정답의 기준만 명확히 알고 있다면 쉽게 풀 수 있는 문제였다.

(이 문제에 대한 정답의 기준은 [10단원]에서 확인하도록 하자)

[0단원]에선 가장 기본적인 "텝스 정답의 기준"을 설명하고, [1~19단원]에서 구체적으로 다룰 것이다.

텝스가 원하는 정답의 기준은 명확히 존재하는데, 이를 파악하기 위해선 각 Part별 유형과 출제 이유에 대해 살펴봐야 할 것이다.

독해 시험에선 이렇게 문제의 유형을 구분하고, 그 중 빈칸 채우기(#1~14)와 주제 찾기(#17~22)를 [텝스의기술 독해 1편]에서 다룬다.

이 유형들에서의 텝스가 원하는 정답을 가장 간단하게 표현해 본다면, "주제문"이라고 할 수 있다. 다시 말해, 1번부터 14번까지와 17번부터 22번까지는 모두 주제문만 파악한다면 분명히 풀 수 있다. 결과적으로 여러분은 이때까지 텝스 영역의 문제를 풀 때, 아무 생각 없이 읽어 내려 갔겠지만, 빈칸 채우기 문제 혹은 주제 찾기 문제에서 요구하는 것은 단 하나였다는 것이다. 또한, 이러한 주제문이 지문 속에 등장하기 때문에, 주제문만 찾아낸 후 정답과 연결하면 되는 것이다.

그러므로 텝스 독해는 2~3문장이면 된다는 것이 당연한 사실이다.

지금까지는 지문 전체의 내용을 읽고 난 후에 주제문을 찾아내는 식의 문제풀이 방식을 택해왔다면, [1단원]부터는 지문 전체를 읽기 전에 주제를 찾는 방법을 학습하게 될 것이고 몇몇 문제들의 문제풀이 속도는 30초 이상 빨라질 것이다.

"주제문"이라고 하면, 진부하다고 느끼는 사람이 많다. 그 이유는 중고등학교 때 선생님들이 항상 "주제문"을 강조하지만 정작 그 주제문을 어떻게 찾아내는지 가르쳐주지 않았기 때문이다. 항상 지문을 해석한 후에 "봐, 이렇게 해석해보니 이 문장이 주제문이 되겠지? 글쓴이가 하고 싶은 말은 이걸 거 아니야~" 라고 하며 넘어가는 식의 교육을 받았기 때문에 주제문의 중요성조차 모르는 것이고, 주제문에 들어가는 여러 가지 법칙들을 이해하지 못하는 것이다.

이 교재에서는 지문을 읽기 전에 주제문만 미리 찾아낼 수 있는 전략들도 소개한다. 또한, 그 문장들을 발견한 후 군더더기 문장들을 배제한 채 문제를 바로 풀 수 있는 전략도 전한다.

그렇지만 오해하지 말길 바란다. 재차 강조하지만, 이 교재는 '요령'을 가르치는 책이 절대 아니다. 주제문과 문제가 원하는 정답의 기준을 관통하는 "원리 원칙대로 풀어나가는 전략"을 세우는 것이다. 요령이라는 것은 불확실성을 수반하기 마련이다. 불확실성을 갖고 최상위권으로 올라갈 수는 없다. 하지만 텝스19 전략을 믿고 따르면 최상위권에 도달할 수 있다. 오로지 요령만을 가르쳐왔다면 어떻게 수도 없이 많은 900점 이상의 학생들을 배출할 수 있었을까?

마지막으로 강조하지만, 본 교재는 "요령"을 가르치지 않는다.

"원리 원칙"을 기반으로 한 문제 풀이 전략 및 점수 극대화 방법을 강의하는 것이다.

텝스의 기술 1권에선 빈칸 채우기 문제(1~14)와 주제 찾기 문제(17~22)를 다룬다.

이 두 가지 유형에선 모든 정답은 주제문에서 나와야 한다는 것을 명심하자.

19개 단원을 학습하면서 기준은 점점 더 명확하게 정립될 것이다.

우선 조금은 막연하더라도, 무조건 정답의 기준은 "주제문"이라고 생각하자.

그리고 [1단원]부터 [19단원]을 모두 학습한 뒤에 다시 [0단원]으로 돌아왔을 때, 또 다른 깨달음을 발견할 것이다.

선택지 두 개 중에 고민 될 때는, 마음속으로 "주제문이 정답의 기준"이라고 외치면 정답이 나올 것이다.

쏘아보기 원리

1

1 쏘아보기 원리

이번 단원이 전체 19개 단원 중에서 가장 중요하다고 볼 수 있다. 모든 문제를 풀 때 적용해야 하는 기술이 "쏘아보기"라는 습관이기 때문이다. 일반적으로 우리는 독해문제를 풀 때 첫 문장부터 차례대로 읽고 문제 풀이로 넘어간다.

모든 문제 풀이 시 일 순위로 첫 문장을 읽는 것은 맞다.

하지만 1순위 전에 0순위로 "쏘아보기"를 해야 한다.

독해 문제풀이 순서 (#1~14, 17~22)

0순위: 쏘아보기

1순위: 첫문장

2순위: ……

3순위: ……

……

✲ 쏘아보기란?

독해 지문이 주어지면 지문을 5초 동안 빠르게 훑는 것이다. 그 5초 동안 "쏘아보기 단서"들에 동그라미 표시를 하면, 그 단서들을 바탕으로 지문에서 가장 중요한 문장들을 파악할 수 있으며, 가장 중요한 문장들 (2~3문장)만 읽고 문제를 풀어낼 수 있다.

– 지문 전체를 읽는 것보다 더 정확하다.

– 지문 전체를 읽는 것보다 더 신속하다.

– 구체적인 "쏘아보기 단서"들은 19단원들에서 익히게 될 것이다.

5초 [지문을 읽는 것이 아니라 훑는 것]

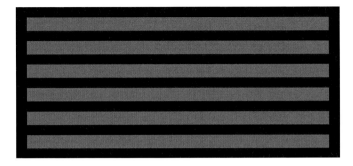

결국, 5초를 투자해서 5초 동안 지문을 읽기보단 빠르게 훑고, 표시된 단서를 바탕으로 독해를 해나가는 것이다. 5초 투자로 그 이상의 시간과 정확도를 얻을 수 있다.

❋ 쏘아보기의 목적은?

쏘아보기의 목적은, 지문에서 가장 중요한 문장들을 찾아내는 데에 있다.

주의 쏘아보기는 오로지 빈칸 채우기 문제와 주제 찾기 문제에만 적용한다.

#1~14, #17~22. 이렇게 20문제는 쏘아보기를 통해 문제를 푸는 것이고, [텝스의 기술, 독해 1편] 에선 오로지 이 20문제만 다룬다. 나머지 4가지 유형의 문제들은 다음 권에서 다루도록 한다.

STRATEGIC
TEPS

II 지문공략법

A단계 | 2~7단원

B단계 | 8~12단원

C단계 | 13~18단원

2

연결어 2개

2 연결어 2개

지금까지 텝스 독해를 할 때는 지문의 내용을 읽고 이해한 후 그 내용을 떠올리며 가장 중요한 부분을 찾아 문제를 풀려고 했을 것이다. 빈칸 채우기 문제 유형과 주제 찾기 유형에서 이러한 독해 방법은 어리석은 것이다. 왜냐하면, 결국 이 문제들에서는 항상 주제만 질문하기 때문이다. 2단원에선 연결어 두 개를 바탕으로 전체 지문에서 2문장만 읽고 문제를 푸는 방법을 소개한다. 2단원 문제를 발견하면 30초 안에 풀 수 있어야 한다.

❈ 쏘아보기 단서

연결어(연결어 뒤에 쉼표로 구분)

ex. However, ~~~~ . In addition, ~~~~~.

※ but은 연결어에서 제외.

❈ 원리 설명

텝스 지문의 길이는 정해져 있다. 이 속에서, 연결어는 칸막이 역할을 한다고 생각하면 된다. 칸막이, 즉, 연결어가 두 개면 칸은 3개가 생기게 되고, 우리는 이 3개의 칸에 우선순위를 메길 수 있다.

예를 들어, However, Additionally 연결어 두 개를 쏘아보기 시 발견했다면, 가장 중요한 부분은 However 뒤, 그다음 중요한 부분은 Additionally 뒤, 그리고 우선순위 3순위는 However 앞부분이 된다.

✱ 문제 풀이

조건: 쏘아보기에서 연결어가 2개 이상 있다면 그 두 개의 연결어를 기준으로 지문 단락 간의 우선순위를 메긴다. 그리고 3개의 칸 중 1순위 부분이 어디인지 확실히 파악한다.

풀이: 지문의 "첫 문장"과 우선순위 "일 순위 문장"을 읽고 선택지로 내려간다면 문제는 풀린다. 이런 원리가 적용되는 이유는 바로 빈칸 채우기 문제와 주제 찾기 문제의 특성 때문이다. 핵심 단서만 파악한다면 20문제 모두 풀 수 있는 것이 빈칸 채우기와 주제 찾기 문제다.

※ 지문에 However가 한 개 보인다고 However 뒤부터 바로 보는 것은 무모한 것이다.
　지문 속에 연결어 2개 이상이 있을 때에만 우선순위에 따라 문장을 읽는다.

우선 30~40초동안 문제를 먼저 풀어보세요.

1. Through the last two decades, the number of animals used in scientific experiments and product testing has more than quadrupled. These animals, more than five million of which are used every year, are mostly rodents like mice, guinea pigs, hamsters and squirrels. While human trials and experiments are becoming more and more expensive and politically sensitive, these animals provide a cost-effective and reasonably human-like alternative to humans. However, increased awareness of animal rights has recently made it much more troublesome to perform testing on animals. Furthermore, the increased demand for rodents as pets caused the animals' prices to rise, making it a much less attractive choice.

Q: What is the topic of the passage?

(a) The problems of testing with animals like rodents

(b) The decreased incentive to use animals like rodents as test subjects

(c) A new legislation concerning scientific testing on animals like rodents

(d) The dangers of human testing and its potential political inconveniences

1. Through the last two decades, the number of animals used in scientific experiments and product testing has more than quadrupled. These animals, more than five million of which are used every year, are mostly rodents like mice, guinea pigs, hamsters and squirrels. While human trials and experiments are becoming more and more expensive and politically sensitive, these animals provide a cost-effective and reasonably human-like alternative to humans. However, increased awareness of animal rights has recently made it much more troublesome to perform testing on animals. Furthermore, the increased demand for rodents as pets caused the animals' prices to rise, making it a much less attractive choice.

Q: What is the topic of the passage?

(a) The problems of testing with animals like rodents

(b) The decreased incentive to use animals like rodents as test subjects

(c) A new legislation concerning scientific testing on animals like rodents

(d) The dangers of human testing and its potential political inconveniences

2. During the decline of Köln Freistadt, the city officials mainly concentrated on law enforcement instead of reviving the city's withering commerce. It was their belief that restoring public order would help the city regain its former prosperity and effectively counter the impending collapse. However, the resulting harsh surveillance and restrictions only caused the city's economy to stagnate even further, since many merchants and craftsmen saw a sharp decrease in floating population, and thus, less profit. Moreover, corruption was rampant among the overly empowered police force, eating away even more of the city's commercial vigor. Therefore, _____ only accelerated the demise of Köln Freistadt.

(a) the commercial inactivity of the merchants and craftsmen

(b) the restoration of public order that put the city back on track

(c) the public order policies imposed to revitalize the city

(d) the corruption of the law enforcement civil workers

2. During the decline of Köln Freistadt, the city officials mainly concentrated on law enforcement instead of reviving the city's withering commerce. It was their belief that restoring public order would help the city regain its former prosperity and effectively counter the impending collapse. However, the resulting harsh surveillance and restrictions only caused the city's economy to stagnate even further, since many merchants and craftsmen saw a sharp decrease in floating population, and thus, less profit. Moreover, corruption was rampant among the overly empowered police force, eating away even more of the city's commercial vigor. Therefore, _____ only accelerated the demise of Köln Freistadt.

(a) the commercial inactivity of the merchants and craftsmen

(b) the restoration of public order that put the city back on track

(c) the public order policies imposed to revitalize the city

(d) the corruption of the law enforcement civil workers

3. The radioactive isotope Tepsium-19 is an uncommon by-product of spontaneous nuclear fission in stars. It is a useful substance which is essential for the operation of the most common types of nuclear fission plants across the world, but is unfortunately extremely rare on Earth. Thus, several powerful nations vied to take a larger share when an abundant reserve of Tepsium-19 was reported to have been discovered on the surface of the Moon in 1969. In addition, global energy conglomerates started lobbying their governments, each competing for an exclusive contract and mining rights. All this fuss subsided, however, when subsequent trips to the moon proved that the alleged Tepsium-19 reserve was found out to be Toefleum-19, which had a similar emission spectrum indistinguishable by existing technologies.

Q: What is the main topic of the passage?

(a) The usefulness of the radioactive isotope Tepsium-19

(b) A disputed rare resource reserve on the surface of the Moon

(c) A worldwide competition for a rare resource that never existed

(d) A historical power struggle between nations and corporate powers

3. The radioactive isotope Tepsium-19 is an uncommon by-product of spontaneous nuclear fission in stars. It is a useful substance which is essential for the operation of the most common types of nuclear fission plants across the world, but is unfortunately extremely rare on Earth. Thus, several powerful nations vied to take a larger share when an abundant reserve of Tepsium-19 was reported to have been discovered on the surface of the Moon in 1969. In addition, global energy conglomerates started lobbying their governments, each competing for an exclusive contract and mining rights. All this fuss subsided, however, when subsequent trips to the moon proved that the alleged Tepsium-19 reserve was found out to be Toefleum-19, which had a similar emission spectrum indistinguishable by existing technologies.

Q: What is the main topic of the passage?

(a) The usefulness of the radioactive isotope Tepsium-19

(b) A disputed rare resource reserve on the surface of the Moon

(c) A worldwide competition for a rare resource that never existed

(d) A historical power struggle between nations and corporate powers

4. Excessive intake of alcohol is very harmful to the human body and can even be lethal in extreme cases. Alcohol in large doses can severely impair vital internal organs such as the liver or the heart. In the pancreas, alcohol causes the production of toxic substances that can lead to pancreatitis, a critical inflammation of blood vessels that prevents proper digestion. There have been, however, studies that suggest moderate consumption of alcohol can be healthy.

Small doses of red wine, for instance, _____.

(a) can be a contributing factor to heart failures

(b) may protect healthy adults from developing coronary heart disease

(c) have been found to increase the risk of developing certain cancers

(d) may release red toxins into the bloodstream

4. Excessive intake of alcohol is very harmful to the human body and can even be lethal in extreme cases. Alcohol in large doses can severely impair vital internal organs such as the liver or the heart. In the pancreas, alcohol causes the production of toxic substances that can lead to pancreatitis, a critical inflammation of blood vessels that prevents proper digestion. There have been, however, studies that suggest moderate consumption of alcohol can be healthy.

Small doses of red wine, for instance, _____.

(a) can be a contributing factor to heart failures

(b) may protect healthy adults from developing coronary heart disease

(c) have been found to increase the risk of developing certain cancers

(d) may release red toxins into the bloodstream

5. Herpes simplex virus accesses human cells, homes on the nucleus and then directs itself into the DNA using high pressure stimulated from a nanometer-scale protein shell known as the capsidpropel. This virus is known to cause infections such as influenza and HIV. However, the Herpes simplex virus is becoming resistant to medicines that aim at the viral proteins, which can instantaneously convert themselves and develop resistance to anti-viral drugs due to genetic mutation. Scientists, thus, are hoping to create a potent drug to reduce the resistance level. So far, they have experimented on mice to create an adequate drug. This could help

_____ .

(a) detect the reason behind the genetic mutation

(b) keep the virus from seeking other viral proteins

(c) develop a new treatment to attack the influenza

(d) prevent the virus from remaining resistant to the drug

5. Herpes simplex virus accesses human cells, homes on the nucleus and then directs itself into the DNA using high pressure stimulated from a nanometer-scale protein shell known as the capsidpropel. This virus is known to cause infections such as influenza and HIV. However, the Herpes simplex virus is becoming resistant to medicines that aim at the viral proteins, which can instantaneously convert themselves and develop resistance to anti-viral drugs due to genetic mutation. Scientists, thus, are hoping to create a potent drug to reduce the resistance level. So far, they have experimented on mice to create an adequate drug. This could help

_____ .

(a) detect the reason behind the genetic mutation

(b) keep the virus from seeking other viral proteins

(c) develop a new treatment to attack the influenza

(d) prevent the virus from remaining resistant to the drug

통념 뒤집기 3

3 통념 뒤집기

텝스 독해에 굉장히 자주 등장하는 유형이 바로 기존 통념을 뒤집으며 새로운 통념을 제시하는 식의 반전 글이다.

예를 들면 이런 글이다. [예전 사람들은 지구가 납작하다고 생각했다. 하지만 콜럼버스는 지구가 둥글다는 것을 밝혀냈다.] 이런 유형들을 발견한다면 30초 안에 풀 수 있어야 한다.

❋ 쏘아보기 단서

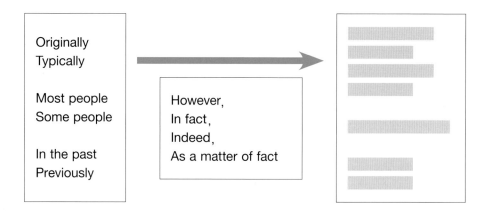

❋ 원리 설명

통념 뒤집기는 텝스에서 크게 두 가지 중 하나로 나타난다.

첫째는 ▓▓▓▓▓▓▓▓▓▓▓▓▓▓▓▓▓▓▓▓▓▓▓▓▓▓▓▓▓▓▓▓▓▓▓ 방식이고,

둘째는 ▓▓▓▓▓▓▓▓▓▓▓▓▓▓▓▓▓▓▓▓▓▓▓▓▓▓▓▓▓▓▓▓▓ 방식의 글이다.

둘 중에 무엇이든지 간에 결국 통념 뒤집기가 파악된 순간, "새로 제시되는 통념"만 파악한다면 정답을 맞힐 수 있다.

"새로 제시되는 통념"은 위에서 다룬 쏘아보기 단서 중 Bpart에 나온 단서들 뒤에 나온다.
[예전 사람들은 지구가 납작하다고 생각했다. 하지만 콜럼버스는 "지구가 둥글다."는 것을 밝혀냈다.] 이 예시에서는 "지구가 둥글다" 만 파악 한다면 정답을 고를 수 있을 것이다. 또한, 이 예시는 시간을 기준으로 통념 뒤집기이기도 하고 (예전, 이제) 대중의 잘못된 통념과 전문가의 의견제시이기도 하다(사람들, 콜럼버스).

(+) However, In fact, Indeed가 두 번째 문장에 나온다면 ░░░░░░░░░░░░░░░░░░
░░░░░░░░░░

❈ 문제 푸는 방법

주제 찾기 유형: 지문 전체에 통념 뒤집기 관련 내용이 나온다면 그것이 무조건 주제가 된다. 예를 들어 In fact가 두 번째 문장에 나오면, 첫 번째 문장과 두 번째 문만 읽고 문제를 풀 수 있는 것이다.

빈칸 채우기 문제: ░░░░░░░░░░░░░░░░░░
░░░░░░░░░░░░░░░

우선 30~40초동안 문제를 먼저 풀어보세요.

1. Recent studies indicate that wiggling one's toes may be much more effective an exercise than previously thought. They claim that just wiggling one's toes for 30 minutes a day can make you lose weight and help prevent diabetes, arthritis and even penile atrophy. A thorough test on 300 individuals of diverse physical conditions proved that an average of 100kcal was lost when they wiggled their toes for 60 minutes, and that it removed about 603mg of harmful chemicals like Tepsium from the body. These astounding numbers exceed even that of weightlifting and jogging. This is an exciting new discovery for those fitness-seekers as no other exercises that can be done on-the-go have been proven to have more efficacy than toe wiggling.

Q: What is the best title for this passage?

(a) The Horrifying Effects of Diabetes, Arthritis and Penile Atrophy

(b) Toe-wiggling Exercise Extremely Helpful for Preventing Various Diseases

(c) A Complete Guide to Burning Fat and Getting Rid of Harmful Chemicals

(d) A New Form of Exercise Found to Have Considerable Effectiveness for Fitness

1. Recent studies indicate that wiggling one's toes may be much more effective an exercise than previously thought. They claim that just wiggling one's toes for 30 minutes a day can make you lose weight and help prevent diabetes, arthritis and even penile atrophy. A thorough test on 300 individuals of diverse physical conditions proved that an average of 100kcal was lost when they wiggled their toes for 60 minutes, and that it removed about 603mg of harmful chemicals like Tepsium from the body. These astounding numbers exceed even that of weightlifting and jogging. This is an exciting new discovery for those fitness-seekers as no other exercises that can be done on-the-go have been proven to have more efficacy than toe wiggling.

Q: What is the best title for this passage?

(a) The Horrifying Effects of Diabetes, Arthritis and Penile Atrophy

(b) Toe-wiggling Exercise Extremely Helpful for Preventing Various Diseases

(c) A Complete Guide to Burning Fat and Getting Rid of Harmful Chemicals

(d) A New Form of Exercise Found to Have Considerable Effectiveness for Fitness

2. It is only recently that people started eating broccoli as food. In fact, the cap of the plant was historically a natural scrub with which the medieval peasants cleaned their latrines.

It is very common for archaeologists to come across broccoli residue in medieval ruins, very often together with fecal matter. Their image as a sanitary device was so well recognized among the peasants that no one dared to try eating it. Similarly, _____.

A 1304 court document in Köln Freistadt describing broccoli chose words like vile, filthy and cursed, indicating even the aristocrats had an aversion for broccoli.

(a) a very negative image of broccoli prevailed among the aristocrats

(b) other organic materials like sea sponge was used for sanitary purposes

(c) aristocrats did have some different thoughts about broccoli and its tastes

(d) broccoli began to be considered somewhat edible from the 14th century onwards

2. It is only recently that people started eating broccoli as food. In fact, the cap of the plant was historically a natural scrub with which the medieval peasants cleaned their latrines.

It is very common for archaeologists to come across broccoli residue in medieval ruins, very often together with fecal matter. Their image as a sanitary device was so well recognized among the peasants that no one dared to try eating it. Similarly, _____.

A 1304 court document in Köln Freistadt describing broccoli chose words like vile, filthy and cursed, indicating even the aristocrats had an aversion for broccoli.

(a) a very negative image of broccoli prevailed among the aristocrats

(b) other organic materials like sea sponge was used for sanitary purposes

(c) aristocrats did have some different thoughts about broccoli and its tastes

(d) broccoli began to be considered somewhat edible from the 14th century onwards

3. Many people, when they picture the Tasty Mango Islands, think of an island country full of romance and breathtaking scenery. However, this is quite contrary to reality. The island has been dealing with an extreme overpopulation crisis since it was first established. In fact, the problem has penetrated the island to such an extent that it has become acceptable and even recommended to walk on people's shoulders when one becomes immobilized in an overcrowded place. The Tasty Mango Island government has been coming up with various measures to fight the problem, but so far none of them has effectively alleviated the problem. The truth is, the island is a stifling pack of tourists and residents with nothing but people's head to see.

Q: What is the main topic of the passage?

(a) The Tasty Mango Island government's policies to counter the overpopulation

(b) The reality of Tasty Mango Islands contrasted to a common misconception

(c) Reasons that the Tasty Mango Islands is no longer what people used to know

(d) Customs that the Island residents have developed adapting to their environment

3. Many people, when they picture the Tasty Mango Islands, think of an island country full of romance and breathtaking scenery. However, this is quite contrary to reality. The island has been dealing with an extreme overpopulation crisis since it was first established. In fact, the problem has penetrated the island to such an extent that it has become acceptable and even recommended to walk on people's shoulders when one becomes immobilized in an overcrowded place. The Tasty Mango Island government has been coming up with various measures to fight the problem, but so far none of them has effectively alleviated the problem. The truth is, the island is a stifling pack of tourists and residents with nothing but people's head to see.

Q: What is the main topic of the passage?

(a) The Tasty Mango Island government's policies to counter the overpopulation

(b) The reality of Tasty Mango Islands contrasted to a common misconception

(c) Reasons that the Tasty Mango Islands is no longer what people used to know

(d) Customs that the Island residents have developed adapting to their environment

BASIC

4. Prior to 1879, when the light bulb was invented by the famous Thomas Edison, activities that might seem ordinary to us were practically impossible to perform at night. With the great modern marvel, the light bulb, which provided much needed light in the darkness of night, people were able to go out for dinner, sleep at a later period, and enjoy other leisure activities that were previously impossible. People were enthralled at the fact that light bulbs

_____.

(a) allowed daily routines to be performed at nighttime

(b) could be modified to the more effective fluorescent bulbs

(c) could finally enhance the quality of movies

(d) were released at cheap prices

4. Prior to 1879, when the light bulb was invented by the famous Thomas Edison, activities that might seem ordinary to us were practically impossible to perform at night. With the great modern marvel, the light bulb, which provided much needed light in the darkness of night, people were able to go out for dinner, sleep at a later period, and enjoy other leisure activities that were previously impossible. People were enthralled at the fact that light bulbs

_____.

(a) allowed daily routines to be performed at nighttime

(b) could be modified to the more effective fluorescent bulbs

(c) could finally enhance the quality of movies

(d) were released at cheap prices

5. When one tries to hatch a baby chick at home, using a Styrofoam box can be an effective solution. However, individuals should still keep in mind that Styrofoam boxes are not the same as ordinary cardboard boxes, and so should be avoided during certain hours. This is because Styrofoam boxes impede the proper flow of air. The inside of the box gets heated during the morning hours, which might negatively influence the egg condition for hatching. Therefore, the Styrofoam box should _____.

(a) be used at night when the temperature is relatively low

(b) determine the optimal temperature of the day

(c) be used at all times when hatching a baby chick at home

(d) be cut into pieces of equal size

5. When one tries to hatch a baby chick at home, using a Styrofoam box can be an effective solution. However, individuals should still keep in mind that Styrofoam boxes are not the same as ordinary cardboard boxes, and so should be avoided during certain hours. This is because Styrofoam boxes impede the proper flow of air. The inside of the box gets heated during the morning hours, which might negatively influence the egg condition for hatching. Therefore, the Styrofoam box should _____.

(a) be used at night when the temperature is relatively low

(b) determine the optimal temperature of the day

(c) be used at all times when hatching a baby chick at home

(d) be cut into pieces of equal size

4

예시, 나열

4 예시, 나열

이번 단원에서 다루게 될 내용은 크게 3가지다.

첫째는 지문에 등장하는 예시와 관련된 글, 둘째는 지문에 등장하는 나열과 관련된 글, 그리고 마지막으로는 Such라는 단어가 등장하는 글. 이렇게 3가지와 관련하여 접근법을 익힐 것이다. 이번 단원 또한 상당히 많이 등장하는 내용인 만큼 확실히 숙지하도록 한다.

�֍ 쏘아보기 단서

1. For example, For instance
2. ▮▮▮▮▮▮▮▮▮▮▮▮▮▮▮▮▮
3. Such, Such as

✖ 원리 설명

1. For example과 For instance는 지문에서 핵심 내용에 대한 예시가 나타났음을 암시한다. 다시 말해 For example이 지문 중간에 등장하면 For example 아래로는 중요하지 않은 내용이고, 결국 For example의 앞 1~2문장이 중요해지는 것이다. 텝스 독해 지문의 한정된 공간을 예시까지 들어가며 하는 것은 그만큼 중요하다는 것이다.

2. 나열된다는 것은 어떠한 범주에 있는 대상들을 늘어서 설명하고 있다. 문제를 푸는 데 필요한 것은 그 범주가 무엇인지 뿐이지, 범주 안에 속하는 내용물 하나하나 다 볼 필요가 없다.

3. Such라는 것은 용도는 두 가지가 있다.
    (1) Such : ▮▮▮▮▮▮▮▮▮▮▮▮▮▮▮▮▮▮▮▮▮▮▮▮▮
    (2) Such as : ▮▮▮▮▮▮▮▮▮▮▮▮▮▮▮▮▮▮▮▮▮▮▮

✳ 문제 푸는 방법

1. For example, For instance. 쏘아보기 시 발견된다면 단서 바로 앞 문장이 주제문이다. 단, 예외가 하나 있는데, For example 앞 문장이 This로 시작하는 경우다. (꼬리의 꼬리물기 단원 참고) [첫 문장 + For example 앞 문장] ⋯▶ 문제풀이

2. ▨▨

3. Such가 발견된다면 as가 있는지 없는지 파악해야 한다. Such as가 보이면 ▨▨▨▨▨을 봐야 하고 Such가 있다면 ▨▨▨▨에 집중하자.

www.teps19.com

1. Iberian Stone Axes of the Paleolithic were made by chipping and cracking rocks by whatever means possible, until the desired shape was achieved. However, a closer inspection reveals that, despite the crude crafting method, the craftsmen who made these axes were masterfully in control of their methods. Just about all of them found within one region seem to share surprisingly identical shapes, suggesting the crafting process was not all that chaotic.

   For example, the Altamira Axes, excavated in the Altamira Cave in Spain, have a common shape which is shared across all 455 axe heads which comprised the collection, with all of them having identical cuts and chipped-off sections of practically the same shape. The truth is that Paleolithic craftsmen _____.

   (a) were not far behind the Neolithic tool-crafting techniques

   (b) were in fairly good control of their crafting techniques

   (c) created advanced cutting tools just by chipping and cracking

   (d) were the most advanced in the Iberian peninsula, like in the Altamira

1. Iberian Stone Axes of the Paleolithic were made by chipping and cracking rocks by whatever means possible, until the desired shape was achieved. However, a closer inspection reveals that, despite the crude crafting method, the craftsmen who made these axes were masterfully in control of their methods. Just about all of them found within one region seem to share surprisingly identical shapes, suggesting the crafting process was not all that chaotic.

   For example, the Altamira Axes, excavated in the Altamira Cave in Spain, have a common shape which is shared across all 455 axe heads which comprised the collection, with all of them having identical cuts and chipped-off sections of practically the same shape. The truth is that Paleolithic craftsmen _____.

   (a) were not far behind the Neolithic tool-crafting techniques

   (b) were in fairly good control of their crafting techniques

   (c) created advanced cutting tools just by chipping and cracking

   (d) were the most advanced in the Iberian peninsula, like in the Altamira

2. Köln Freistadt was the primary commercial center of northeastern Europe from the 11th century to its fall in 1405. Although the city had only 520 permanent residents, there remains the ruins of three large cathedrals, seven minor chapels, two plazas and numerous commercial and residential structures(houses, stores, stables, etc.), ninety-seven inns and hotels, seven guard barracks and 40km of city walls and a massive government building, all of which is speculated to have accommodated over 300,000 merchants from all over Europe who supported the city's economy. As a result, the city is considered to _____ out of all known cities either in history or in the contemporary times.

(a) have been the most commerce-dependent city
(b) have had the most lucrative commercial goods
(c) a dream for archaeologists seeking fame and fortune
(d) have been by far the most populous city

2. Köln Freistadt was the primary commercial center of northeastern Europe from the 11th century to its fall in 1405. Although the city had only 520 permanent residents, there remains the ruins of three large cathedrals, seven minor chapels, two plazas and numerous commercial and residential structures(houses, stores, stables, etc.), ninety-seven inns and hotels, seven guard barracks and 40km of city walls and a massive government building, all of which is speculated to have accommodated over 300,000 merchants from all over Europe who supported the city's economy. As a result, the city is considered to _____ out of all known cities either in history or in the contemporary times.

(a) have been the most commerce-dependent city
(b) have had the most lucrative commercial goods
(c) a dream for archaeologists seeking fame and fortune
(d) have been by far the most populous city

3. During the colonial period of America, Puritans, a group of Christians promoting an austere lifestyle, were predominant. Whenever its members would not follow in their footsteps, the Puritan leaders either banished or publically punished them. For example, if an individual was to involve oneself with gluttony-excessive eating and drinking-he or she would be forced to suffer public punishment in the form of a scaffold, which humiliated the offender in front of his or her peers. These types of punishments _____.

(a) led to the early demise of the Puritanism

(b) encouraged rebellious behaviors among citizens

(c) were against the ideals of Puritan leaders

(d) helped sustain a strict Puritan ideology

3. During the colonial period of America, Puritans, a group of Christians promoting an austere lifestyle, were predominant. Whenever its members would not follow in their footsteps, the Puritan leaders either banished or publically punished them. For example, if an individual was to involve oneself with gluttony-excessive eating and drinking-he or she would be forced to suffer public punishment in the form of a scaffold, which humiliated the offender in front of his or her peers. These types of punishments _____.

(a) led to the early demise of the Puritanism

(b) encouraged rebellious behaviors among citizens

(c) were against the ideals of Puritan leaders

(d) helped sustain a strict Puritan ideology

4. Joanna Carroll has just published a novel that _____.

This book completely reveals the malicious torture tactics that were used upon the women who had been suspected of being witches and being related to witchcraft. Women of the 17th century who were charged of witchcraft were forced to suffer from humiliation and excruciating pain of burning or ripping of the skin. The book's depiction of such preposterous behavior is extremely graphic, enabling the readers to almost feel the pain from the torture.

(a) vividly sheds light on ludicrous behaviors conducted during witch trials

(b) somehow justifies the conducts of torture during the 17th century

(c) gives attention to different types of torture present in history

(d) tries to understand the underlying meaning of the charges of witchcraft

4. Joanna Carroll has just published a novel that _____.

This book completely reveals the malicious torture tactics that were used upon the women who had been suspected of being witches and being related to witchcraft. Women of the 17th century who were charged of witchcraft were forced to suffer from humiliation and excruciating pain of burning or ripping of the skin. The book's depiction of such preposterous behavior is extremely graphic, enabling the readers to almost feel the pain from the torture.

(a) vividly sheds light on ludicrous behaviors conducted during witch trials

(b) somehow justifies the conducts of torture during the 17th century

(c) gives attention to different types of torture present in history

(d) tries to understand the underlying meaning of the charges of witchcraft

BASIC

www.teps19.com

5. Chlorophyll, a pigment found in the chloroplasts of plant cells, gives plants their green color. It is where photosynthesis takes place, gathering all the sunlight and dioxide, which is crucial for the health of a plant. Similar to chlorophyll are different colored-pigments, such as xanthophylls and carotenoids, which reflect the color of the plant. These pigments are used in photosynthesis as well although they appear in lesser quantities than green chlorophylls. For example, a leaf prevented from receiving sunlight would not be green due to the lack of chlorophyll for photosynthesis.

Q: What is the main topic of the passage?
(a) The process of photosynthesis
(b) Why leaves reflect colors of different pigments
(c) The elements that make plants green
(d) The effects of chlorophyll on plants

5. Chlorophyll, a pigment found in the chloroplasts of plant cells, gives plants their green color. It is where photosynthesis takes place, gathering all the sunlight and dioxide, which is crucial for the health of a plant. Similar to chlorophyll are different colored-pigments, such as xanthophylls and carotenoids, which reflect the color of the plant. These pigments are used in photosynthesis as well although they appear in lesser quantities than green chlorophylls. For example, a leaf prevented from receiving sunlight would not be green due to the lack of chlorophyll for photosynthesis.

Q: What is the main topic of the passage?
(a) The process of photosynthesis
(b) Why leaves reflect colors of different pigments
(c) The elements that make plants green
(d) The effects of chlorophyll on plants

5

빈칸 위치 접근법

5 빈칸 위치 접근법

빈칸 채우기 문제와 주제 찾기는 공통점이 있었다.

둘 다 문제를 풀기 위해선 결정적 단서 딱 하나가 필요했는데, 그것은 바로 핵심 문장이었다. 그렇다면, 빈칸 채우기 문제의 빈칸에 들어가는 내용 또한 중요한 내용이 들어가는 것이다. 빈칸이 뚫려있는 문제와 빈칸이 없는 문제 모두 쏘아보기를 하는데, 빈칸이 뚫려있다면 그 위치는 엄청난 의미를 담고 있다. 텝스 시험에서 빈칸의 위치는 어떻게 중요한지 생각해보자.

❋ 쏘아보기 단서

빈칸의 위치는 크게 3가지로 나뉜다.

1. 첫 문장에 위치한 빈칸
2. 중간에 위치한 빈칸
3. 마지막 문장에 위치한 빈칸

여기서 중요한 것이 있는데, 텝스 시험에서 "2. 중간에 위치한 빈칸" 는 시험에 나오질 않는다. 시험에서 정말 가끔가다 나오는 경우가 한가지 있는데, 그것은 빈칸이 뒤에서 두 번째 문장에 있는 경우다. 그래서 빈칸의 위치는 다시 3가지로 재분류할 수 있겠다.

1. 첫 문장에 위치한 빈칸
2. 뒤에서 두 번째 문장에 위치한 빈칸
3. 마지막 문장에 위치한 빈칸

✤ 원리 설명

들어가기에 앞서 기본 전제가 하나 있다. 빈칸에 들어가는 내용은 아무 문장이나 들어가는 것이 아니라, 주제와 깊은 관련이 있는 중요한 문장에 빈칸을 뚫어놓는 것이다.

즉, 빈칸의 위치가 어디 있든지 간에, 빈칸에 들어가는 내용은 지문에서 중요한 문장이라는 것이다.

1. 첫 문장의 역할은 크게 두 개 중 하나다. 첫째는 도입식 내용이고, 두 번째는 주제문 제시다. 앞서 다룬 빈칸에 들어가는 내용에 대한 전제를 살펴보면 빈칸이 첫 문장에 위치할 때 빈칸의 내용이 도입식 내용이 될 수 없다. 따라서 빈칸이 첫 문장에 위치하면 첫 번째 문장이 무조건 주제문이다.
2. 빈칸이 뒤에서 두 번째에 있을 때엔 문제가 굉장히 어려울 확률이 높다. 그리고 이 모든 경우엔 █████████에 문제 풀이를 위한 핵심 단서가 들어간다.
3. 빈칸이 마지막에 있을 때엔 가장 마지막 문장의 역할을 확실히 파악하기 어렵다. 그래서 포괄적인 접근법이 필요하다.

✤ 문제 풀이 방법

1~14번 문제를 풀기 시작할 땐 문제마다 빈칸에 체크를 해야 한다. 빈칸 채우기 문제를 풀 땐 빈칸에 체크 표시를 하는 습관을 들이자.

1. 첫 문장에 위치한 빈칸

2. 뒤에서 두 번째 문장에 위치한 빈칸

3. 마지막 문장에 위치한 빈칸

우선 30~40초동안 문제를 먼저 풀어보세요.

1. Dear Andy,

I am writing to update you on the admission process for the last spot at Benjamin Franklin Academy. So far, the number of candidates remaining has been reduced to three. The academic qualities of you and the other two candidates are outstanding and would be more than befitting for the school. As the number of students that can be admitted is very limited, we unfortunately will be selecting only one candidate. Regardless of the result, please remember that all of you are _____. The finalized decision will be announced next Monday.

Regards, Justin Blake

Admission Administrator, Benjamin Franklin Academy

(a) students whose schools are going to miss

(b) very likely to become the dearest members of our faculty

(c) wonderful candidates who will be accepted with scholarships

(d) exceptional applicants who would be valuable additions to the school

1. Dear Andy,

I am writing to update you on the admission process for the last spot at Benjamin Franklin Academy. So far, the number of candidates remaining has been reduced to three. The academic qualities of you and the other two candidates are outstanding and would be more than befitting for the school. As the number of students that can be admitted is very limited, we unfortunately will be selecting only one candidate. Regardless of the result, please remember that all of you are _____. The finalized decision will be announced next Monday.

Regards, Justin Blake

Admission Administrator, Benjamin Franklin Academy

(a) students whose schools are going to miss

(b) very likely to become the dearest members of our faculty

(c) wonderful candidates who will be accepted with scholarships

(d) exceptional applicants who would be valuable additions to the school

2. _____ is utterly natural for most scientists now and then, but it was not a concern for Marie Curie and her husband. Soon after Marie Curie finally succeeded in creating the decigram of pure radium, the treatment to cancer using this matter was newly discovered. A boom of industries using radium exhilarated the price of Curie's finding. However, she and her husband published the process on extracting radium for the public quoting that the radium belonged to the people. Her insistence on free accessibility to radium brought about developments in creating cures to cancer.

(a) Funding research for adequate experiments

(b) Requesting for intellectual rights for monetary reasons

(c) Patenting scientific discoveries

(d) Delivering the results through publications

2. _____ is utterly natural for most scientists now and then, but it was not a concern for Marie Curie and her husband. Soon after Marie Curie finally succeeded in creating the decigram of pure radium, the treatment to cancer using this matter was newly discovered. A boom of industries using radium exhilarated the price of Curie's finding. However, she and her husband published the process on extracting radium for the public quoting that the radium belonged to the people. Her insistence on free accessibility to radium brought about developments in creating cures to cancer.

(a) Funding research for adequate experiments

(b) Requesting for intellectual rights for monetary reasons

(c) Patenting scientific discoveries

(d) Delivering the results through publications

3. _____ has not been confirmed by anyone. A number of people, however, claim that they started in the early 20th century, when an ice cream stand owner in Coney Island, New York, was selling ice cream at the State Fair. Around noon, when the sun was scorching hot, he ran out of paper cups to serve his ice cream. Not knowing what to do, the ice cream salesman went next door to a waffle salesman and asked him to make cups made of waffles. The ice cream salesman started serving his ice cream in the new cup, and surprisingly, people fell in love with the new "Waffle Cone," and therefore, a new way of serving ice cream was invented.

(a) Why Waffle Cones taste so delicious

(b) Why paper cups were so ineffective

(c) How Waffle Cones came into existence

(d) The negative effects of Waffle Cones

3. _____ has not been confirmed by anyone. A number of people, however, claim that they started in the early 20th century, when an ice cream stand owner in Coney Island, New York, was selling ice cream at the State Fair. Around noon, when the sun was scorching hot, he ran out of paper cups to serve his ice cream. Not knowing what to do, the ice cream salesman went next door to a waffle salesman and asked him to make cups made of waffles. The ice cream salesman started serving his ice cream in the new cup, and surprisingly, people fell in love with the new "Waffle Cone," and therefore, a new way of serving ice cream was invented.

(a) Why Waffle Cones taste so delicious

(b) Why paper cups were so ineffective

(c) How Waffle Cones came into existence

(d) The negative effects of Waffle Cones

4. When consumers go to grocery stores to buy their beef for a family dinner, they may be upset that the price of the beef is too high. At the same time, when farmers bring beef to the market they wish that price of the beef was even higher. These views are not surprising: buyers always want to pay less, but sellers _____. Could a "right price" exist for beef from the standpoint of society as a whole?

(a) want more beef

(b) want less beef

(c) always want to be paid more

(d) always want to be paid less

4. When consumers go to grocery stores to buy their beef for a family dinner, they may be upset that the price of the beef is too high. At the same time, when farmers bring beef to the market they wish that price of the beef was even higher. These views are not surprising: buyers always want to pay less, but sellers _____. Could a "right price" exist for beef from the standpoint of society as a whole?

(a) want more beef

(b) want less beef

(c) always want to be paid more

(d) always want to be paid less

5. The human rights committee is in agreement to the liberation of political prisoners from China during the 1950s. Continuing to hold the politicians captive, who were forcefully arrested without a fair trial, only diminishes the significance of human rights and exudes a notorious reputation among the international society. On the other hand, discharging these prisoners may prompt wreckage in social order. Maintaining strong governmental control will become even harder. However, the committee remains firm that the state should _____.

(a) proceed with the movement to free political prisoners

(b) allow the argument between the government and civilians

(c) reward participants in undertaking the human rights plan

(d) substantially decrease governmental power

5. The human rights committee is in agreement to the liberation of political prisoners from China during the 1950s. Continuing to hold the politicians captive, who were forcefully arrested without a fair trial, only diminishes the significance of human rights and exudes a notorious reputation among the international society. On the other hand, discharging these prisoners may prompt wreckage in social order. Maintaining strong governmental control will become even harder. However, the committee remains firm that the state should _____.

(a) proceed with the movement to free political prisoners

(b) allow the argument between the government and civilians

(c) reward participants in undertaking the human rights plan

(d) substantially decrease governmental power

편지글

6 편지글

[6단원] 편지글과 [7단원] 광고글은 내용별로 나눠서 정리된 단원들이다. 이 두 가지 유형 외엔 따로 내용적인 부분에 초점을 맞출 필요가 없지만, [6단원]과 [7단원]만큼은 따로 정리해 둘 필요가 있다. 또한, 이 두 가지 유형은 전체 시험에서 비중이 20% 정도가 되는 만큼 확실히 정리해 둔다면 빠른 시간 내에 문제를 풀어나갈 수 있을 것이다.

❋ 쏘아보기 단서

부정: However, ⬛⬛⬛⬛⬛⬛⬛⬛, ⬛⬛⬛⬛⬛⬛⬛⬛

긍정: Therefore, So, In particular

부탁: ⬛⬛⬛⬛⬛⬛⬛⬛⬛⬛

공지글: Announce, Please, Thank you

기타

❋ 원리 설명

편지글에는 입에 발린 소리가 등장하는 경우가 많다. 편지글의 핵심, 그리고 문제를 풀기 위해서 필요한 부분은 입에 발린 소리가 절대 아니다. 주제와 관련 없는 부분은 바로 건너뛸 수 있어야 한다. 그래서 위에 나와 있는 쏘아보기 단서들을 눈여겨 봐야 하는 것이다. 위에 명시된 단서들이 형식적인 이야기에서 편지의 핵심 내용으로 건너가는 중요한 단서들이다.

⁘ 문제 풀이

편지글이라는 것을 파악한 순간 쏘아보기 단서들을 잡아야 한다. 쏘아보기 단서들을 기준으로 글의 성격을 예측하고, 단서가 들어가는 문장을 읽어야 한다.
예를 들어 쏘아보기 중에 지문 중간에 Therefore이 나왔다는 것은 편지의 내용 자체가 긍정적인 내용일 것이라는 것이고, Therefore이 등장하는 문장이 핵심 문장일 것이다.

BASIC

www.teps19.com

우선 30~40초동안 문제를 먼저 풀어보세요.

1. Dear Ms. Clementz,

   The University of St. Glenzow _____. We wish to inform you that your application was exceptional, and therefore will be accepting you to our exchange student program. Please send us your student visa and the confirmation application from your school. If you require more information, or wish to change your plans for the exchange program, email us via our university website st.glenzow@edu.org

   (a) is excited to invite you to its annual summer camp

   (b) would like to welcome you to a new semester

   (c) wants to hear more from you

   (d) will be recruiting new professors

1. Dear Ms. Clementz,

   The University of St. Glenzow _____. We wish to inform you that your application was exceptional, and therefore will be accepting you to our exchange student program. Please send us your student visa and the confirmation application from your school. If you require more information, or wish to change your plans for the exchange program, email us via our university website st.glenzow@edu.org

   (a) is excited to invite you to its annual summer camp

   (b) would like to welcome you to a new semester

   (c) wants to hear more from you

   (d) will be recruiting new professors

2. To all Jamestown residents

   Sightings of a mentally ill man holding a rifle has been reported several times over the last few days. It is not yet clear who the man may be and how he gained access to his rifle, but it is suspected that he is the man who escaped from the mental asylum last week. The police say they are currently searching for this crazy man, and the situation is under control. Fortunately, there have not been any shootings or accidents, but the police warns that his rifle is apparently loaded and cocked, and the mental asylum records show that he is a retired veteran army officer with a condition of paranoia. Please stay indoors and keep your doors locked until the madman is captured and arrested by the local police.

Clyfford de Stijl

Town Mayor

Q: What is the purpose of the announcement?

(a) To collect more evidence for tracking down an insane man.

(b) To warn people not to leave their houses because of a danger.

(c) To ask people to cooperate with the police's search mission.

(d) To investigate where the insane man obtained his rifle.

2. To all Jamestown residents

Sightings of a mentally ill man holding a rifle has been reported several times over the last few days. It is not yet clear who the man may be and how he gained access to his rifle, but it is suspected that he is the man who escaped from the mental asylum last week. The police say they are currently searching for this crazy man, and the situation is under control. Fortunately, there have not been any shootings or accidents, but the police warns that his rifle is apparently loaded and cocked, and the mental asylum records show that he is a retired veteran army officer with a condition of paranoia. Please stay indoors and keep your doors locked until the madman is captured and arrested by the local police.

Clyfford de Stijl

Town Mayor

Q: What is the purpose of the announcement?

(a) To collect more evidence for tracking down an insane man.

(b) To warn people not to leave their houses because of a danger.

(c) To ask people to cooperate with the police's search mission.

(d) To investigate where the insane man obtained his rifle.

3. To: US Army Station Camp Henry Logistics Team

Captain Clarice Merleau-ponty

I have realized today that the number of rifles that was relocated to our base was different from what the documents say. My men and I have rechecked the numbers several times, but it seems clear that 7 of the M16A3 rifles we were supposed to receive have gone missing. I am afraid that it may have been taken by hijackers, while the cargo was passing by Jamestown. Sources suggest that _____, which enabled this to happen despite very strict protocols. I request that you alert the military police immediately, before this matter becomes any more serious.

Regards

Lieutenant Commander Michael Foucault

US Army Station Camp Huxley Logistics Team

(a) the hijackers may be very familiar with our security procedures

(b) the hijackers are headed to the military police department

(c) the military police has not yet been informed about the incident

(d) the press may know something about this incident already

3. To: US Army Station Camp Henry Logistics Team

Captain Clarice Merleau-ponty

I have realized today that the number of rifles that was relocated to our base was different from what the documents say. My men and I have rechecked the numbers several times, but it seems clear that 7 of the M16A3 rifles we were supposed to receive have gone missing. I am afraid that it may have been taken by hijackers, while the cargo was passing by Jamestown. Sources suggest that _____, which enabled this to happen despite very strict protocols. I request that you alert the military police immediately, before this matter becomes any more serious.

Regards

Lieutenant Commander Michael Foucault

US Army Station Camp Huxley Logistics Team

(a) the hijackers may be very familiar with our security procedures

(b) the hijackers are headed to the military police department

(c) the military police has not yet been informed about the incident

(d) the press may know something about this incident already

4. Dear Student

We would first like to congratulate you on being selected to this year's student of the year. Your academic achievements and philanthropic spirit is no doubt exemplar for all of our students. Therefore, we are delighted to invite you to the 2013 Jamestown-Surley Dinner Party, where you will meet, dine and talk with renowned academics from diverse fields. Furthermore, you will be asked to give the starting speech for the event, which is an honor rarely given to students. Please do not miss this precious life opportunity; we assure you that it will become one of the most unforgettable moments in your entire life.

Frederick Paritzche

Professor, California Institute of Technology

Q: What is the main idea of the letter?

(a) The student has been nominated for the student of the year award

(b) The college will be holding a meeting between famous academics this year

(c) The student in question has been invited to a very special event

(d) The 2013 Jamestown College Dinner Party will be very memorable

4. Dear Student

We would first like to congratulate you on being selected to this year's student of the year. Your academic achievements and philanthropic spirit is no doubt exemplar for all of our students. Therefore, we are delighted to invite you to the 2013 Jamestown-Surley Dinner Party, where you will meet, dine and talk with renowned academics from diverse fields. Furthermore, you will be asked to give the starting speech for the event, which is an honor rarely given to students. Please do not miss this precious life opportunity; we assure you that it will become one of the most unforgettable moments in your entire life.

Frederick Paritzche

Professor, California Institute of Technology

Q: What is the main idea of the letter?

(a) The student has been nominated for the student of the year award

(b) The college will be holding a meeting between famous academics this year

(c) The student in question has been invited to a very special event

(d) The 2013 Jamestown College Dinner Party will be very memorable

5. All class-4 personnel contaminated by the microorganism SCP-9983 must consult the facility quarantine officer before leaving the premises. Under the facility quarantine protocol, all associated individuals will undergo a decontamination procedure free of charge, and will be provided with a week's dose of antibacterial tablets. The quarantine department assures you that none of the crew will suffer permanent illness due to the microorganism, and promises insurance for those whose symptoms persist. Please note, however, anyone who violates the protocol will be eliminated.

Q: What is the announcement mainly about?

(a) The actions that will be taken against those who violate the protocol.

(b) Reasons why the facility quarantine protocol should be adhered to.

(c) The medication that is to be issued to contaminated personnel.

(d) A mandatory quarantine protocol for associated staff

5. All class-4 personnel contaminated by the microorganism SCP-9983 must consult the facility quarantine officer before leaving the premises. Under the facility quarantine protocol, all associated individuals will undergo a decontamination procedure free of charge, and will be provided with a week's dose of antibacterial tablets. The quarantine department assures you that none of the crew will suffer permanent illness due to the microorganism, and promises insurance for those whose symptoms persist. Please note, however, anyone who violates the protocol will be eliminated.

Q: What is the announcement mainly about?

(a) The actions that will be taken against those who violate the protocol.

(b) Reasons why the facility quarantine protocol should be adhered to.

(c) The medication that is to be issued to contaminated personnel.

(d) A mandatory quarantine protocol for associated staff

광고글 7

7 광고글

[6단원]과 함께 형식이 정해져 있는 단원이다. 형식이 정해져 있는 만큼 정답의 기준도 명확하다. 절대로 고민하는 일이 있어서는 안 되는 글의 유형이 바로 광고글 유형이다. "제품 광고니까 당연히 이것도 정답이 될 수 있고 저것도 답이 될 수 있지 않나?"라는 생각을 하며 문제 풀이 시간이 길어진 경험이 있다면, 이 단원에서 확실한 기준을 확립하는 것이 중요할 것이다.

❈ 쏘아보기 단서

We, Our product

❈ 원리 설명

광고글은 크게 세 가지로 나뉜다고 생각하면 된다.

X. 광고하는 제품/서비스, Y. 그 제품/서비스의 장점, Z. 광고성 멘트

X는 그 제품이 무엇인지 설명하는 부분으로, Samsung Galaxy S5 라는 제품을 홍보하는 것이라면, "Samsung Galaxy S5"가 아닌, "휴대폰"으로 생각하면 된다.

Y는 중요한 부분인데, 지문 중간에 장점이 나열된다. 여러 장점이 나열되는 것이 아니라 정확히 하나의 장점만 제시되는 형태다. 그리고 마지막 문장에 Z 광고성 멘트가 등장한다.

✽ 문제 풀이

문제를 풀 때 X (광고되고 있는 제품)이 무엇인지, 그리고 Y (장점 1개)를 파악하면 된다. 1번을 파악하자마자 지문 전체를 나열[4단원] 부분 읽듯이 빠르게 훑으며 장점만 파악하면 된다.

광고성 문제의 특징은 정답 또한 X 혹은 Y에서 나온다는 것이다. 만약 광고글 중에 고민 되는 보기가 있다면 그땐 다시 광고글 기준을 떠올려 본다면 정답을 고를 수 있을 것이다.

우선 30～40초동안 문제를 먼저 풀어보세요.

1. Do you hate having to choose what to wear every day? Would you rather prefer 5 more minutes of sleep than having to decide what to wear? Then just call ClothesFit today for a 7-day free trial of preselected clothes every morning. We offer competitive monthly expenses, discounts for high schoolers, and trustworthy courteous service. Sign a monthly contract with us before January 6th and get 15% off. Don't _____ just call ClothesFit at 466-0542!

(a) lose 5 minutes of your sleep

(b) give your clothes selection another thought

(c) hesitate any longer

(d) worry about the trendiness of the style selection

1. Do you hate having to choose what to wear every day? Would you rather prefer 5 more minutes of sleep than having to decide what to wear? Then just call ClothesFit today for a 7-day free trial of preselected clothes every morning. We offer competitive monthly expenses, discounts for high schoolers, and trustworthy courteous service. Sign a monthly contract with us before January 6th and get 15% off. Don't _____ just call ClothesFit at 466-0542!

(a) lose 5 minutes of your sleep

(b) give your clothes selection another thought

(c) hesitate any longer

(d) worry about the trendiness of the style selection

2. Looking for _____? You should come to see the Boston Celtics play at the TD Garden located in downtown Boston! Ticket prices range from 50 dollars to 3000 dollars. Every seat is provided with an adequate amount of beer for you and snacks for you and your kids. The exciting atmosphere will be a great experience for the kids and you will be able to blow off some steam. Visit www.tdgarden.co.kr for more information.

(a) an exciting experience for you and your kids

(b) something to do on the weekend

(c) a place to eat beer and watch basketball

(d) a nice treat for your wife

2. Looking for _____? You should come to see the Boston Celtics play at the TD Garden located in downtown Boston! Ticket prices range from 50 dollars to 3000 dollars. Every seat is provided with an adequate amount of beer for you and snacks for you and your kids. The exciting atmosphere will be a great experience for the kids and you will be able to blow off some steam. Visit www.tdgarden.co.kr for more information.

(a) an exciting experience for you and your kids

(b) something to do on the weekend

(c) a place to eat beer and watch basketball

(d) a nice treat for your wife

3. With turnitin.com _____. We digitalize the classroom so that the students can submit their assignments through the internet and also get feedback in a fast and efficient manner. We also provide a state of the art plagiarism prevention system: providing the exact percentage of how much a certain paper matches the words of others. With this system, professors and teachers can have a much easier time picking out the dishonest students in the classroom.

(a) students can have fun learning

(b) teachers have a more important role than before

(c) virtual schools can replace actual schools

(d) education from the teaching perspective becomes efficient

3. With turnitin.com _____. We digitalize the classroom so that the students can submit their assignments through the internet and also get feedback in a fast and efficient manner. We also provide a state of the art plagiarism prevention system: providing the exact percentage of how much a certain paper matches the words of others. With this system, professors and teachers can have a much easier time picking out the dishonest students in the classroom.

(a) students can have fun learning

(b) teachers have a more important role than before

(c) virtual schools can replace actual schools

(d) education from the teaching perspective becomes efficient

4. Interested in working in the most comfortable working environment for you? Work-at-home jobs provide you with a convenient working environment, freedom of attire, and many more advantages. HomeWork will arrange you with companies with working home opportunities according to your career. As soon as you receive our service, you will be discovering yourself free from the intense working atmosphere. Simply leave it to HomeWork and we will bring your work to your home.

Q: What is the advertisement mainly about?

(a) An opportunity to work at home

(b) How to balance out the pros and cons of working at home

(c) A company that introduces work-at-home jobs

(d) A service that provides positions at a prestigious corporations

4. Interested in working in the most comfortable working environment for you? Work-at-home jobs provide you with a convenient working environment, freedom of attire, and many more advantages. HomeWork will arrange you with companies with working home opportunities according to your career. As soon as you receive our service, you will be discovering yourself free from the intense working atmosphere. Simply leave it to HomeWork and we will bring your work to your home.

Q: What is the advertisement mainly about?

(a) An opportunity to work at home

(b) How to balance out the pros and cons of working at home

(c) A company that introduces work-at-home jobs

(d) A service that provides positions at a prestigious corporations

5. With the service at Heckscher, you are completely free from the pain of termites. You simply make a call and relax for a while as our trained professionals eradicate even the miniscule trace of termites with FDA approved chemicals and high quality equipment. Extra services are available for 30 days within the previous session and other options, including the type of chemicals or quick-call service without additional cost, are also available. There are no better options for termite treatments than Heckschers! Call us at 602-4529-0016 right now. Free yourself from the unnecessary pain.

Q: What is mainly being advertised?

(a) A chemical engineering company

(b) A service center that augments the problem of termites

(c) An insect controlling company

(d) A family business run by the Heckschers

5. With the service at Heckscher, you are completely free from the pain of termites. You simply make a call and relax for a while as our trained professionals eradicate even the miniscule trace of termites with FDA approved chemicals and high quality equipment. Extra services are available for 30 days within the previous session and other options, including the type of chemicals or quick-call service without additional cost, are also available. There are no better options for termite treatments than Heckschers! Call us at 602-4529-0016 right now. Free yourself from the unnecessary pain.

Q: What is mainly being advertised?

(a) A chemical engineering company

(b) A service center that augments the problem of termites

(c) An insect controlling company

(d) A family business run by the Heckschers

STRATEGIC
TEPS

문장 기호

INTERMEDIATE

8 문장 기호

문장 기호라는 것은 독자에게 글 읽기를, 화자에게 글쓰기를 편하게 만들어 주는 도구로써 효과적인 의사소통을 돕는다. 문장 기호 속엔 여러 가지 강조점들과 유의점들이 암시되어 있는데, 시험마다 이 문장 기호의 사용을 통일시켜 사용한다. 토플에도 문장 기호로 유추할 수 있는 부분이 있고, 토익도 그러한 부분이 많고, 텝스에도 많은 문장 기호들이 전체 지문의 전개 방향을 보여주기 때문에 쏘아보기 시 발견된다면 내용을 어느 정도 예측할 수 있을 것이다.

❈ 쏘아보기 단서

?

!

:

,

" "

( )

Italics

❈ 원리 설명 및 문제풀이 방법

?. 물음표는 개수가 하나인지 두 개 이상인지 에 따라서 접근법이 나뉜다.

물음표가 하나 있을 때엔 속으로,   라고 외쳐야 한다.

물음표가 2개 이상이면, 물음이 들어가는 문장들은

!. 느낌표는 중요한 부분을 강조하기 위해 사용될 때도 있지만 광고글이나 편지글에서 자신의 의견을 전할 때 사용되는 경우도 있다. 느낌표가 나온다면 느낌표가 등장하는 그 문장을 가볍게 한번 읽어보는 것이 좋다.

www.teps19.com

: . 콜론도 꽤 중요한 문장 기호 중 하나다. 콜론 뒤에 등장하는 부분을 ▨▨▨▨▨▨▨▨
▨▨▨▨▨▨▨▨▨▨

예외: 콜론 뒤에 나열이 돼 있는 경우만 특별히 예외다.

" ". 따옴표. 따옴표의 역할은 두 개 중 하나다. ▨▨▨과 ▨▨▨가 있다. ▨▨▨은 예시의 용도로
사용된다고 생각하면 된다. ▨▨▨는 단어 1~3개 정도를 강조하기 위해 사용되는 것이며 주로
"생소개념(0단원 참고)"이 따옴표 속에 강조된다. 따옴표가 인용 하고 있다면 인용되는 부분은
읽지 않고 그 앞에 부분을 자세히 보도록 하고, 따옴표가 강조의 역할을 하고 있다면 강조되고
있는 단어가 무엇인지 확인할 필요가 있다.

, 쉼표. ▨▨▨▨▨▨▨▨▨▨▨▨▨▨▨▨▨▨▨▨▨▨▨▨

이탤릭체. 텝스에서 이탤릭체는 서적 제목을 나타낼 때가 가장 많다. 쏘아보기에서 이탤릭체엔
별다른 의미를 둘 필요는 없지만, ▨▨▨▨▨▨▨▨▨▨ 할 때 이탤릭체는 중요하다.

1. Have you ever wondered how they can tell the speed of a car right after it moves through the speed gun? Radar guns are positioned on the road, which send out waves or signals at fixed frequencies towards the ball when it is moving towards the target. These signals hit the car and bounce back to the radar detector. These guns work on a principle known as the Doppler Effect. The Doppler Effect describes the change in the frequency of a wave that occurs when the source and receiver are in relative motion. The frequency of the wave increases as the source and receiver approach each other. The radar gun measures the shift in the frequency of a wave to calculate the velocity.

Q: What is the main idea of the passage?

(a) A radar gun records the changes in the frequency of a wave

(b) Speeding cars are able to calculate the speed of waves.

(c) The Doppler Effect takes relative motion into consideration.

(d) Speed measurement makes use of the Doppler Effect

1. Have you ever wondered how they can tell the speed of a car right after it moves through the speed gun? Radar guns are positioned on the road, which send out waves or signals at fixed frequencies towards the ball when it is moving towards the target. These signals hit the car and bounce back to the radar detector. These guns work on a principle known as the Doppler Effect. The Doppler Effect describes the change in the frequency of a wave that occurs when the source and receiver are in relative motion. The frequency of the wave increases as the source and receiver approach each other. The radar gun measures the shift in the frequency of a wave to calculate the velocity.

Q: What is the main idea of the passage?

(a) A radar gun records the changes in the frequency of a wave

(b) Speeding cars are able to calculate the speed of waves.

(c) The Doppler Effect takes relative motion into consideration.

(d) Speed measurement makes use of the Doppler Effec

2. Don't you think it would be fascinating to _____?

In fact, this is actually possible if you visit our website, freetrips.org. Starting today, we will post information that would require customer opinion about travel journeys: just take 2 minutes to fill out the form, and you will be given 2 free tickets to Hawaii! Make your wish come true by visiting our website. This is your ultimate opportunity to gain an experience that you would never be able to have elsewhere.

(a) play games all day

(b) go on a special vacation for free

(c) share your hobby online

(d) study abroad

2. Don't you think it would be fascinating to _____?

In fact, this is actually possible if you visit our website, freetrips.org. Starting today, we will post information that would require customer opinion about travel journeys: just take 2 minutes to fill out the form, and you will be given 2 free tickets to Hawaii! Make your wish come true by visiting our website. This is your ultimate opportunity to gain an experience that you would never be able to have elsewhere.

(a) play games all day

(b) go on a special vacation for free

(c) share your hobby online

(d) study abroad

3. When consumers go to grocery stores to buy their beef for a family dinner, they may be upset that the price of the beef is too high. At the same time, when farmers bring beef to the market they wish that price of the beef was even higher. These views are not surprising: buyers always want to pay less, but sellers _____. Could a "right price" exist for beef from the standpoint of society as a whole?

(a) want more beef

(b) want less beef

(c) always want to be paid more

(d) always want to be paid less

3. When consumers go to grocery stores to buy their beef for a family dinner, they may be upset that the price of the beef is too high. At the same time, when farmers bring beef to the market they wish that price of the beef was even higher. These views are not surprising: buyers always want to pay less, but sellers _____. Could a "right price" exist for beef from the standpoint of society as a whole?

(a) want more beef

(b) want less beef

(c) always want to be paid more

(d) always want to be paid less

4. The SAT scores of the students in my school were all ranked within the top one percent of the nation. Beneath that, however, the desires of the higher group were not much different from those of the lower 99 percent. These overachieving students, whose daily routines never allowed for any significant pastimes, had piles of magazines and game CDs under their beds, Justin Hoover, Starcraft and Playboy were all a part of their hidden treasures. It was as if, despite having no time or apparent desire whatsoever for these mediocre hobbies, they were driven by the same instinct as any other student: to seek something fun.

Q: What is the passage mainly about?

(a) A prestigious school that the writer attended

(b) A reason why we seek fun things even when we are busy

(c) A surprising similarity between the top students and the rest

(d) The hidden treasures of overachieving students within the top one percent

4. The SAT scores of the students in my school were all ranked within the top one percent of the nation. Beneath that, however, the desires of the higher group were not much different from those of the lower 99 percent. These overachieving students, whose daily routines never allowed for any significant pastimes, had piles of magazines and game CDs under their beds, Justin Hoover, Starcraft and Playboy were all a part of their hidden treasures. It was as if, despite having no time or apparent desire whatsoever for these mediocre hobbies, they were driven by the same instinct as any other student: to seek something fun.

Q: What is the passage mainly about?

(a) A prestigious school that the writer attended

(b) A reason why we seek fun things even when we are busy

(c) A surprising similarity between the top students and the rest

(d) The hidden treasures of overachieving students within the top one percent

5. Statistics provided by UN Development Program reveal that while the United States has always been a capitalist country, the _____. Over several decades, the situation exacerbated. By 2007, the average after-tax income of the top 1 percent had reached $1.3 million, but that of the bottom 20 percent amounted to only $17,800. The richest 20 percent earns in total after tax more than the bottom 80 percent combined. These outcomes challenge the general perception we have of the United States as the "Land of Equal Opportunity".

(a) everyone receives equal opportunity

(b) extent of inequality in society actually expanded

(c) democratic notions of peace were settled deeply in society

(d) country was reluctant in caring about the environment

5. Statistics provided by UN Development Program reveal that while the United States has always been a capitalist country, the _____. Over several decades, the situation exacerbated. By 2007, the average after-tax income of the top 1 percent had reached $1.3 million, but that of the bottom 20 percent amounted to only $17,800. The richest 20 percent earns in total after tax more than the bottom 80 percent combined. These outcomes challenge the general perception we have of the United States as the "Land of Equal Opportunity".

(a) everyone receives equal opportunity

(b) extent of inequality in society actually expanded

(c) democratic notions of peace were settled deeply in society

(d) country was reluctant in caring about the environment

양괄식

9 양괄식

[9단원]은 의외로 굉장히 단순한 단원이다. 이미 양괄식 구조에 대해 들어 온 학생들도 많을 것이지만 그만큼 중요한 단원이기 때문에 추가하였다. 또한, 양괄식에 대한 정확한 개념을 알고 있는 학생은 많지 않기 때문에, 다시 정리해보는 단원이다. 양괄식 구조를 쏘아보기 단계에서 잘 맞춰보고, 기준에 들어맞지 않을 때는 양괄식 구조라고 생각하면 안 된다.

✽ 쏘아보기 단서–

마지막 빈칸, So, Therefore, Thus (마지막 문장)

✽ 원리 설명

양괄식 구조는 글의 중심 내용이 첫머리와 끝 부분에 반복하여 나타나는 문단 구성 방식이다.
하지만 9단원에서 양괄식이라는 개념을 재 정의 하겠다.
텝스의 기술에서 말하는 양괄식 구조란, "문제를 풀기 위해 첫 문장과 마지막 문장이 필요한 구조" 다. 이런 구조를 발견만 할 수 있다면 첫 문장과 마지막만 읽고 문제를 풀면 되는 것이다.

✽ 문제 풀이

1. 첫문장이 도입식 문장이 아니고

2. 빈칸이 마지막 문장에 있는데

3. ▨▨▨▨▨▨▨▨ 로 시작하고

4. 지문 중간에 ▨▨▨ 가 따로 없을 때

지문은 "양괄식 구조"로 분류된다.

이런 조건에 맞는 문제가 있다면 무조건 첫 문장과 마지막 문장을 읽는다.

우선 30~40초동안 문제를 먼저 풀어보세요.

1. During the Great Depression in the 1920s, the United States was actually _____

_____. As the economy was under drastic conditions, people were sincerely wishing
to divert their attention from the disastrous situation to more entertainment and excitement.
Thus, classic films including Frankenstein and Gone with the Wind had made their debuts and
received great affection from the public during this time.

(a) turning its attention to films

(b) going under a change particularly in the theater industry

(c) going through major progress economically

(d) globally emerged as a trendsetter in cultural aspects

1. During the Great Depression in the 1920s, the United States was actually _____

_____. As the economy was under drastic conditions, people were sincerely wishing
to divert their attention from the disastrous situation to more entertainment and excitement.
Thus, classic films including Frankenstein and Gone with the Wind had made their debuts and
received great affection from the public during this time.

(a) turning its attention to films

(b) going under a change particularly in the theater industry

(c) going through major progress economically

(d) globally emerged as a trendsetter in cultural aspects

2. In the book the Last Lecture, Randy Pausch _____. Randy is a professor at Carnegie Mellon and is diagnosed with pancreatic cancer, which only gives him 3 to 6 months to live. He gradually starts the process of letting go of the little and irrelevant things in life such as fighting with his wife over who does the laundry or worrying about the stains on his car. He, thus, realizes how important spending time with family and friends is and how meaningless and time-consuming some of his previous jobs have been.

(a) explains how cancer influenced his family

(b) realizes the value of time in one's life

(c) bemoans being cursed with pancreatic cancer

(d) rediscovers his love for life

2. In the book the Last Lecture, Randy Pausch _____. Randy is a professor at Carnegie Mellon and is diagnosed with pancreatic cancer, which only gives him 3 to 6 months to live. He gradually starts the process of letting go of the little and irrelevant things in life such as fighting with his wife over who does the laundry or worrying about the stains on his car. He, thus, realizes how important spending time with family and friends is and how meaningless and time-consuming some of his previous jobs have been.

(a) explains how cancer influenced his family

(b) realizes the value of time in one's life

(c) bemoans being cursed with pancreatic cancer

(d) rediscovers his love for life

3. Recently an energy drink called the "Energy Bottle" has been on sale in local malls. Containing the ingredient Glyzerintine, the drink is known to keep a person awake for 26 hours. For students and businessmen who have limited amount of time and an intensive amount of workload, it may seem efficient to boost up work productivity by consuming the drink. Nevertheless, the World Health Organization recently published a research report claiming that Glyzerintine is toxic, and may increase the risk of heart disease. Therefore taking this into account, people _____.

(a) should be more cautious of having the energy drink

(b) should not stay up for 26 hours

(c) are advised to drink coffee instead

(d) should study the benefits of "Energy Bottle"

3. Recently an energy drink called the "Energy Bottle" has been on sale in local malls. Containing the ingredient Glyzerintine, the drink is known to keep a person awake for 26 hours. For students and businessmen who have limited amount of time and an intensive amount of workload, it may seem efficient to boost up work productivity by consuming the drink. Nevertheless, the World Health Organization recently published a research report claiming that Glyzerintine is toxic, and may increase the risk of heart disease. Therefore taking this into account, people _____.

(a) should be more cautious of having the energy drink

(b) should not stay up for 26 hours

(c) are advised to drink coffee instead

(d) should study the benefits of "Energy Bottle"

4. Korean high schools have only themselves to blame if they find that their students are not attentive during the morning. Most competitive high schools in Korea require students to come to school by 7:40 in the morning. To come to school by this time, students usually need to wake up at six or even earlier. Most studies conducted by psychologists and sleep experts claim that our brain is not fully awake and active by this time. Therefore a better strategy would be to

_____.

(a) change the schools into night schools

(b) provide more take home assignments

(c) wake up earlier than six o' clock

(d) start school at a later time

4. Korean high schools have only themselves to blame if they find that their students are not attentive during the morning. Most competitive high schools in Korea require students to come to school by 7:40 in the morning. To come to school by this time, students usually need to wake up at six or even earlier. Most studies conducted by psychologists and sleep experts claim that our brain is not fully awake and active by this time. Therefore a better strategy would be to

_____.

(a) change the schools into night schools

(b) provide more take home assignments

(c) wake up earlier than six o' clock

(d) start school at a later time

5. Many teenagers who are into building muscle want to take supplements. These include protein shakes, BCAAs, multi-vitamins, fish oil and etc. All these are dedicated to help building muscle faster and to provide more energy for workouts. Or so they say. There are plenty of evidence and studies that show these supplements to be useless. So it is no wonder that parents are

_____.

(a) working out at a less efficient rate than their children.

(b) joining their kids in purchasing these products.

(c) hesitant when it comes to buying these products for their children

(d) concerned about health issues from consuming supplements

5. Many teenagers who are into building muscle want to take supplements. These include protein shakes, BCAAs, multi-vitamins, fish oil and etc. All these are dedicated to help building muscle faster and to provide more energy for workouts. Or so they say. There are plenty of evidence and studies that show these supplements to be useless. So it is no wonder that parents are

_____.

(a) working out at a less efficient rate than their children.

(b) joining their kids in purchasing these products.

(c) hesitant when it comes to buying these products for their children

(d) concerned about health issues from consuming supplements

10

연결어 뉘앙스

10 연결어 뉘앙스

영작 전문가들은 개별 연결어들의 뉘앙스를 따로 정리해서 문단 전개의 특성에 맞춰 사용하도록 교육을 받는다. 자신이 표현하고자 하는 내용을 독자에게 제대로 전달하기 위하여 사용하는 도구가 바로 "연결어"라는 것이다. 우리는 이런 연결어들의 뉘앙스를 미리 파악하면 뒤따를 내용의 예측이 가능한 것이다. 또한, 연결어들이 나온다는 것은 특정 부분이 강조 되고 있다는 뜻이므로 주제가 될 확률이 높아진다는 것도 참고해야 한다.

❋ 쏘아보기 단서

따로 없음.
지문을 읽는 과정에서 발견되는 모든 연결어.

❋ 원리 설명

특정 연결어들은 문장 내에서 A라는 부분을 부정하면서 B를 긍정하곤 한다.
시험에서 이러한 연결어들이 나온다면 A를 피해 B를 읽어야 하기도 하지만, B에 강조된다는 것을 알아야 한다.
또한, 지문 내에서 같은 부분이 이중으로 강조된다면 그 부분이 주제가 되는 것이다. "이중 강조는 주제."를 기억하자.
만약 연결어 뉘앙스[10단원]에 해당하는 연결어가 첫 문장에 나온다면 그것이 주제문이 되는 것이다.

❋ 문제 풀이

쏘아보기가 아닌 문제 풀이 단계에서 지문을 읽을 때 연결어가 등장한다면 B를 표시하고 읽는다. 정답에 B 부분이 연결 될 가능성이 크기 때문이다.

While A, B.

Although A, B.

Despite A, B.

Even though A, B.

✔ 이중 강조는 주제.

INTERMEDIATE

www.teps19.com

우선 30~40초동안 문제를 먼저 풀어보세요.

1. While the so-called "dumb" phones are disappearing quickly, some other electronic gadgets are disappearing even faster. Digital cameras, portable gaming console, PDAs and mp3 players have almost disappeared off the market since 2010, and they may become completely obsolete by the next few years. The leading factor contributing to their demise is the sheer multi-functionality of smart phones. With their phones becoming more versatile and compact than ever, people are no longer feeling the need for bulky separate devices.

   Q: What is the passage mainly about?

   (a) The inconvenience of using separate devices

   (b) The demise of numerous electronic devices

   (c) The disappearance of dumb phones from the market

   (d) The versatility and compactness of smartphones

1. While the so-called "dumb" phones are disappearing quickly, some other electronic gadgets are disappearing even faster. Digital cameras, portable gaming console, PDAs and mp3 players have almost disappeared off the market since 2010, and they may become completely obsolete by the next few years. The leading factor contributing to their demise is the sheer multi-functionality of smart phones. With their phones becoming more versatile and compact than ever, people are no longer feeling the need for bulky separate devices.

   Q: What is the passage mainly about?

   (a) The inconvenience of using separate devices

   (b) The demise of numerous electronic devices

   (c) The disappearance of dumb phones from the market

   (d) The versatility and compactness of smartphones

2. Tobacco Gum was prevalent in Major League Baseball in the United States during the mid to late 20th century, even though it _____. As people were finding out that these tobacco products could lead to cancer, and when the children, after seeing their favorite players use chewing tobacco, were trying them out, Major League officials started banning the use of these products. The players, in the end, chose bubble gum, which was both healthier and more visually appealing.

(a) was mainly consumed in Europe

(b) caused no health hazards for the players

(c) contained many carcinogenic substances

(d) was against the will of the fans

2. Tobacco Gum was prevalent in Major League Baseball in the United States during the mid to late 20th century, even though it _____. As people were finding out that these tobacco products could lead to cancer, and when the children, after seeing their favorite players use chewing tobacco, were trying them out, Major League officials started banning the use of these products. The players, in the end, chose bubble gum, which was both healthier and more visually appealing.

(a) was mainly consumed in Europe

(b) caused no health hazards for the players

(c) contained many carcinogenic substances

(d) was against the will of the fans

3. The head coach of the 2010 Korean speed skating national team, Leonardo Kim, has long been praised for his _____. Even though he spent most of his skating career on the Korean national team where he earned three gold medals, it was his agility and creative skating skills that considerably influenced the world of speed skating. For instance, in the 1998 Olympic Games, Leonardo first disclosed his cross-legging skating style which is still the fastest known way to skate in a corner and is used by all skaters in speed skating.

    (a) outstanding contributions to the development of speed skating

    (b) medals for victories during the 1998 Olympic Games

    (c) construction of the Korean Olympics ice rink stadium

    (d) coaching skills he showed after his retirement as a professional

3. The head coach of the 2010 Korean speed skating national team, Leonardo Kim, has long been praised for his _____. Even though he spent most of his skating career on the Korean national team where he earned three gold medals, it was his agility and creative skating skills that considerably influenced the world of speed skating. For instance, in the 1998 Olympic Games, Leonardo first disclosed his cross-legging skating style which is still the fastest known way to skate in a corner and is used by all skaters in speed skating.

    (a) outstanding contributions to the development of speed skating

    (b) medals for victories during the 1998 Olympic Games

    (c) construction of the Korean Olympics ice rink stadium

    (d) coaching skills he showed after his retirement as a professional

4. The phenomenon of group conformity is surprisingly prevalent in various occasions. Despite the fact that an individual knew the answer to a simple test question with certainty, the subject ended up providing the wrong answer to go along with the crowd. Psychologically, people actually convince themselves that they are thinking what the group is thinking. The tendency is highly probable when in great uncertainty. Also, the feeling of assimilation plays a crucial role in such behavioral inclination. People's primary motivation is to be liked and accepted by others and their greatest fear is to be different and alienated.

Q: What is the passage mainly about?

(a) The feeling of fear that affects one's decision-making process

(b) An experiment conducted on an excluded subject

(c) Reasons why an individual had the wrong answer

(d) The attitude and action of the majority having profound influence on individuals

4. The phenomenon of group conformity is surprisingly prevalent in various occasions. Despite the fact that an individual knew the answer to a simple test question with certainty, the subject ended up providing the wrong answer to go along with the crowd. Psychologically, people actually convince themselves that they are thinking what the group is thinking. The tendency is highly probable when in great uncertainty. Also, the feeling of assimilation plays a crucial role in such behavioral inclination. People's primary motivation is to be liked and accepted by others and their greatest fear is to be different and alienated.

Q: What is the passage mainly about?

(a) The feeling of fear that affects one's decision-making process

(b) An experiment conducted on an excluded subject

(c) Reasons why an individual had the wrong answer

(d) The attitude and action of the majority having profound influence on individuals

5. Although it may seem difficult to sleep when you suffer from insomnia, _____.
Various simple measures will help you. For instance, try counting sheep, or drink a cup of warm
milk before you lie down. Think about complex mathematical equations that would make your
brain fried. If it still doesn't work, take a thick academic book and read it for about 5 minutes.
You would find your eyelids slowly getting heavier.

(a) you should find a comfortable bed to help you sleep

(b) there are ways to make falling asleep easier

(c) you should always be more active during the day

(d) sufficient rest is important for a healthy body

5. Although it may seem difficult to sleep when you suffer from insomnia, _____.
Various simple measures will help you. For instance, try counting sheep, or drink a cup of warm
milk before you lie down. Think about complex mathematical equations that would make your
brain fried. If it still doesn't work, take a thick academic book and read it for about 5 minutes.
You would find your eyelids slowly getting heavier.

(a) you should find a comfortable bed to help you sleep

(b) there are ways to make falling asleep easier

(c) you should always be more active during the day

(d) sufficient rest is important for a healthy body

11

부정 후엔 긍정

11 부정 후엔 긍정

이번 단원 "부정 후엔 긍정"은 A is not B but C라는 간단한 구문에서 출발하는 것이다. 이 간단한 구문이 텝스 지문 한 문장 한 문장에 쓰이기도 하지만 텝스 지문의 전체 구조에 여러 문장에 거쳐서 나타나기도 한다. 각각의 경우에 어떻게 문제풀이를 해 나가야 하는지 감만 잡는다면 시간 절약이 확실히 될 것이다.

⁂ 쏘아보기 단서

쏘아보기 단서는 따로 없음.
문장 내에서 Not only, But also

⁂ 원리 설명

1. 문장 내에 A is not B but C. 라는 구조는 A=C 라는 메시지를 전달하고 싶은 것이다. 그 속에 B를 부정함으로써 C를 강조하는 것이다.
   A is not B but C.
   A는 B가 아니라 C이다.
   A는 B보다 C이다.
   A is not only B, but also C.
2. 지문을 통틀어서 이런 구조가 나타날 수 있다. A is not B but C라는 것은 결국 A is not B. ______ 이렇게 두 개로 나뉠 수 있다. 그렇다면 첫 문장에 A is not B.라는 글이 나온다면, 지문 중반부 혹은 후반부에 ______가 나올 것으로 예측할 수 있다. 또한, 결국 A is not B라는 것은 중요하지 않은 것이니 오로지 ______만 파악하면 주제는 파악 되는 것이다. "A는 B가 아니다."라는 것을 주제로 하는 글은 없을 것이다.

✻ 문제 풀이

원리 설명에서 다뤘다시피 B를 발견하는 순간 C가 있을 것을 인지하고 바로 C를 찾아 나서야 한다.

연습문제

우선 30~40초동안 문제를 먼저 풀어보세요.

1. Most grievances about parents from their children don't concern perceptible inequalities, like quitting a job so they can help their children with their homework or studies or giving them much freedom, such as a big allowance, a lot of spare time, and easy access to the internet. What they complain about most is communication, saying that their parents do not try to understand what they say. Most children, as a matter of fact, feel affection not when they receive much freedom, but rather when they feel understood.

Q: What is the main idea of the passage?

(a) Parents are much better communicators than children

(b) Children want more freedom from their parents

(c) Children understand that parents want to communicate

(d) Children want to be better understood by their parents

1. Most grievances about parents from their children don't concern perceptible inequalities, like quitting a job so they can help their children with their homework or studies or giving them much freedom, such as a big allowance, a lot of spare time, and easy access to the internet. What they complain about most is communication, saying that their parents do not try to understand what they say. Most children, as a matter of fact, feel affection not when they receive much freedom, but rather when they feel understood.

Q: What is the main idea of the passage?

(a) Parents are much better communicators than children

(b) Children want more freedom from their parents

(c) Children understand that parents want to communicate

(d) Children want to be better understood by their parents

2. During the decline of Köln Freistadt, the city officials mainly concentrated on law enforcement instead of reviving the city's withering commerce. It was their belief that restoring public order would help the city regain its former prosperity and effectively counter the impending collapse. However, the resulting harsh surveillance and restrictions only caused the city's economy to stagnate even further, since many merchants and craftsmen saw a sharp decrease in floating population, and thus, less profit. Moreover, corruption was rampant among the overly empowered police force, eating away even more of the city's commercial vigor. Therefore, _____ only accelerated the demise of Köln Freistadt.

(a) the commercial inactivity of the merchants and craftsmen

(b) the restoration of public order that put the city back on track

(c) the public order policies imposed to revitalize the city

(d) the corruption of the law enforcement civil workers

2. During the decline of Köln Freistadt, the city officials mainly concentrated on law enforcement instead of reviving the city's withering commerce. It was their belief that restoring public order would help the city regain its former prosperity and effectively counter the impending collapse. However, the resulting harsh surveillance and restrictions only caused the city's economy to stagnate even further, since many merchants and craftsmen saw a sharp decrease in floating population, and thus, less profit. Moreover, corruption was rampant among the overly empowered police force, eating away even more of the city's commercial vigor. Therefore, _____ only accelerated the demise of Köln Freistadt.

(a) the commercial inactivity of the merchants and craftsmen

(b) the restoration of public order that put the city back on track

(c) the public order policies imposed to revitalize the city

(d) the corruption of the law enforcement civil workers

3. During the decline of Köln Freistadt, the city officials mainly concentrated on law enforcement instead of reviving the city's withering commerce. It was their belief that restoring public order would help the city regain its former prosperity and effectively counter the impending collapse. However, the resulting harsh surveillance and restrictions only caused the city's economy to stagnate even further, since many merchants and craftsmen saw a sharp decrease in floating population, and thus, less profit. Moreover, corruption was rampant among the overly empowered police force, eating away even more of the city's commercial vigor.

Therefore, _____ only accelerated the demise of Köln Freistadt.

(a) the commercial inactivity of the merchants and craftsmen

(b) the restoration of public order that put the city back on track

(c) the public order policies imposed to revitalize the city

(d) the corruption of the law enforcement civil workers

3. During the decline of Köln Freistadt, the city officials mainly concentrated on law enforcement instead of reviving the city's withering commerce. It was their belief that restoring public order would help the city regain its former prosperity and effectively counter the impending collapse. However, the resulting harsh surveillance and restrictions only caused the city's economy to stagnate even further, since many merchants and craftsmen saw a sharp decrease in floating population, and thus, less profit. Moreover, corruption was rampant among the overly empowered police force, eating away even more of the city's commercial vigor.

Therefore, _____ only accelerated the demise of Köln Freistadt.

(a) the commercial inactivity of the merchants and craftsmen

(b) the restoration of public order that put the city back on track

(c) the public order policies imposed to revitalize the city

(d) the corruption of the law enforcement civil workers

4. Military boot camp is, in a way, a cycle. Newly incoming soldiers enter boot camp every month. Then, they are put into a series of training that will push them to their limits not only physically but also mentally and emotionally. But that doesn't mean they don't have a good time because they form bonds with all the people around them. These bonds are very powerful and so a lot of soldiers are motivated to come back to base camp and work as drill officers. Because of this,

_____.

(a) forming a sense of camaraderie in the boot camp is the most important.

(b) many trainees become a different person once they leave the camp

(c) there is always an adequate supply of people in boot camp

(d) the number of incoming soldiers increase annually

4. Military boot camp is, in a way, a cycle. Newly incoming soldiers enter boot camp every month. Then, they are put into a series of training that will push them to their limits not only physically but also mentally and emotionally. But that doesn't mean they don't have a good time because they form bonds with all the people around them. These bonds are very powerful and so a lot of soldiers are motivated to come back to base camp and work as drill officers. Because of this,

_____.

(a) forming a sense of camaraderie in the boot camp is the most important.

(b) many trainees become a different person once they leave the camp

(c) there is always an adequate supply of people in boot camp

(d) the number of incoming soldiers increase annually

5. The Korean _____. Samsung Electronics is playing a big role in this area, with its innovative ideas shaping the lifestyles of the ordinary people. Its recent release of the Galaxy 4 Series has been receiving positive appeal not only in the local market, but also in the international market. People now get to enjoy new technologies which make their daily lives more efficient and convenient.

(a) economy is led by a few major IT companies

(b) IT companies are affecting the lives of the global population

(c) government is striving for new ways to develop technology

(d) market is declining due to the recent economic crisis

5. The Korean _____. Samsung Electronics is playing a big role in this area, with its innovative ideas shaping the lifestyles of the ordinary people. Its recent release of the Galaxy 4 Series has been receiving positive appeal not only in the local market, but also in the international market. People now get to enjoy new technologies which make their daily lives more efficient and convenient.

(a) economy is led by a few major IT companies

(b) IT companies are affecting the lives of the global population

(c) government is striving for new ways to develop technology

(d) market is declining due to the recent economic crisis

12 연구내용/결과

12 연구내용/결과

텝스 지문에서 어떤 시험이나 연구 내용이 나온다면, 그 내용의 역할은 정해져 있다.

텝스 문제에서 실제 연구/실험의 내용을 묻진 않는다.

██████은 읽을 필요 없이 오로지 ██████에만 집중하면 되는 것이다. 정말 많이 등장하는 유형이므로 꼭 숙지하도록 한다.

✲ 쏘아보기 단서

Study, Evidence, Survey, Research

~Shows that~

Experimental results

Observed, Found

✲ 원리 설명

연구 내용과 연구 결과라는 것은 비슷한 듯 보이지만 텝스 지문에선 아예 다른 역할을 한다.

██████은 구체적으로 어떤 연구가 진행됐는지 설명하는 부분이다.

반면에 ██████는 어떤 결론이 도출되었는지 보여준다. 정답인 주제는 결론에서 나오고, 결국 정답도 ██████에서 나오는 것이다.

✲ 문제 풀이

결국, 우리는 결과만 필요한 것이니 앞으로 Study/Experiment가 등장한다면 ██████를 찾는 것이 중요하다. ██████은 전혀 중요하지 않다.

우선 30~40초동안 문제를 먼저 풀어보세요.

1. French gourmet and connoisseur Jean Grandetgras proposed the term "amuse-bouche" in 1963 to name the small, bite-sized dishes which became fashionable recently for master chefs to serve before the meal. He observed that the dish was not ordered from the menu by patrons, but often served freely by the chef's choice alone. The custom soon provided an arena of competition for chefs to show their mastery of cooking. Shortly after, the competition resulted in the chefs using the finest ingredients and the most avant-garde of recipes, that the gourmet named it "amuse-bouche", meaning "mouth amuser".

Q: What is the main idea about Amuse-bouche according to the passage?

(a) The Gourmet Jean Grandetgras first coined the term in 1913

(b) An amuse-bouche is cooked and designed according to the diner's wishes

(c) It was observed by the gourmet that amuse-bouche was often neglected by patrons

(d) Amuse-bouche became very high-quality soon after its introduction, due to competition

1. French gourmet and connoisseur Jean Grandetgras proposed the term "amuse-bouche" in 1963 to name the small, bite-sized dishes which became fashionable recently for master chefs to serve before the meal. He observed that the dish was not ordered from the menu by patrons, but often served freely by the chef's choice alone. The custom soon provided an arena of competition for chefs to show their mastery of cooking. Shortly after, the competition resulted in the chefs using the finest ingredients and the most avant-garde of recipes, that the gourmet named it "amuse-bouche", meaning "mouth amuser".

Q: What is the main idea about Amuse-bouche according to the passage?

(a) The Gourmet Jean Grandetgras first coined the term in 1913

(b) An amuse-bouche is cooked and designed according to the diner's wishes

(c) It was observed by the gourmet that amuse-bouche was often neglected by patrons

(d) Amuse-bouche became very high-quality soon after its introduction, due to competition

2. British scientists from the University of Oxford and Cambridge have come to the conclusion that Branch Chain Amino Acids, a supplement often used by bodybuilders for faster muscle growth and recovery, _____. 100 athletes all around England were given BCAAs in the form of pills and their muscle growth was measured over a period of one year. However, the results showed no difference from the muscle growth of the control group which received no such supplements.

(a) can cause liver disease

(b) decrease muscle mass

(c) do not live up to its description

(d) are only effective on women

2. British scientists from the University of Oxford and Cambridge have come to the conclusion that Branch Chain Amino Acids, a supplement often used by bodybuilders for faster muscle growth and recovery, _____. 100 athletes all around England were given BCAAs in the form of pills and their muscle growth was measured over a period of one year. However, the results showed no difference from the muscle growth of the control group which received no such supplements.

(a) can cause liver disease

(b) decrease muscle mass

(c) do not live up to its description

(d) are only effective on women

3. With the city of Seoul trying to reduce toxic water, oysters just might be the answer. Studies conducted by the University of Oxford show that oysters breathe in toxic water and let out relatively cleaner water in whatever environment they are in. Inserting 500 oysters into a body of water the size of Lake Eerie will decrease the toxic level by 4.7% in a time span of three weeks. Experts claim that this is the best way to _____.

(a) deal with Seoul's water pollution and toxic waste-

(b) drive up the toxic level in Seoul

(c) make Lake Eerie clean once and for all

(d) create a safe ecosystem for oysters

3. With the city of Seoul trying to reduce toxic water, oysters just might be the answer. Studies conducted by the University of Oxford show that oysters breathe in toxic water and let out relatively cleaner water in whatever environment they are in. Inserting 500 oysters into a body of water the size of Lake Eerie will decrease the toxic level by 4.7% in a time span of three weeks. Experts claim that this is the best way to _____.

(a) deal with Seoul's water pollution and toxic waste-

(b) drive up the toxic level in Seoul

(c) make Lake Eerie clean once and for all

(d) create a safe ecosystem for oysters

4. A new study suggests that if mothers were to avoid using the microwave, they may have a better chance of preventing cancer in their future children. Researchers, through careful examination of 4000 pregnant women, have concluded that microwaves cause prenatal cancer genes to form in the fetus. They found that every ten minutes of exposure to an operating microwave increases the chance of cancer by one percent. The discovery indicates an evident correlation between microwave exposure and the risk of the future offspring contracting cancer.

Q: What is the passage mainly about?

(a) Microwave exposure can cause infertility in mothers

(b) Microwave ovens increase the risk of cancer in mothers

(c) The need for future children to avoid using the microwave

(d) Exposure to microwaves can increase the chance of cancer in unborn children

4. A new study suggests that if mothers were to avoid using the microwave, they may have a better chance of preventing cancer in their future children. Researchers, through careful examination of 4000 pregnant women, have concluded that microwaves cause prenatal cancer genes to form in the fetus. They found that every ten minutes of exposure to an operating microwave increases the chance of cancer by one percent. The discovery indicates an evident correlation between microwave exposure and the risk of the future offspring contracting cancer.

Q: What is the passage mainly about?

(a) Microwave exposure can cause infertility in mothers

(b) Microwave ovens increase the risk of cancer in mothers

(c) The need for future children to avoid using the microwave

(d) Exposure to microwaves can increase the chance of cancer in unborn children

5. Structural stress in aluminum fuselages cause some of the molecular alignment to become condensed. In other words, the originally linear alignment becomes jagged and irregular when structural force is applied. While this change may harmlessly increase the overall durability of the structure, it eventually causes the tensile strength to deteriorate drastically and become dangerously brittle. A research conducted on crashed aircrafts discovered that aluminum fuselages that suffered from prolonged structural stress absorbed less shock from the impact, resulting in higher casualty counts.

Q: What is the main idea of the passage?

(a) Structural stress sometimes strengthens an aluminum structure in the short term

(b) Structural stress is the main cause of many aircraft crashes

(c) Structural stress is detrimental to the structural safety of a fuselage

(d) Prolonged structural stress can have devastating results unless special caution is
   taken during use

5. Structural stress in aluminum fuselages cause some of the molecular alignment to become condensed. In other words, the originally linear alignment becomes jagged and irregular when structural force is applied. While this change may harmlessly increase the overall durability of the structure, it eventually causes the tensile strength to deteriorate drastically and become dangerously brittle. A research conducted on crashed aircrafts discovered that aluminum fuselages that suffered from prolonged structural stress absorbed less shock from the impact, resulting in higher casualty counts.

Q: What is the main idea of the passage?

(a) Structural stress sometimes strengthens an aluminum structure in the short term

(b) Structural stress is the main cause of many aircraft crashes

(c) Structural stress is detrimental to the structural safety of a fuselage

(d) Prolonged structural stress can have devastating results unless special caution is
   taken during use

STRATEGIC
TEPS

13

동급 나열식

13 동급 나열식

```
┌─────────────────────────────────┐
│   첫 문장 _____ 빈칸 _____ .   │
│                                 │
│   첫째, ~~~~~~~~~~              │
│   둘째, ~~~~~~~~~~              │
│   셋째, ~~~~~~~~~~              │
└─────────────────────────────────┘
```

첫 문장에 빈칸이 들어가 있고, 지문 나머지엔 첫째, 둘째, 셋째라는 동급 구조로 진행이 되는 지문 구조를 "동급 나열식 구조"라고 한다.

❋ 쏘아보기 단서

First, Second, Third, Lastly,

Also,

Another,

These

In addition, Furthermore

❋ 원리 설명

쏘아보기 시 First, Second, Third, Lastly, Also, Another, These, In addition, Furthermore이 나온다면 동급 나열식 구조라는 것을 파악할 수 있다. 동급 나열식이라는 것이 파악 된다면 결국 A/B/C 구조를 나눠서 표시한다.

✽ 문제 풀이

A/B/C 중의 하나(가장 짧은 것)를 먼저 읽고, 선택지로 가서 정답이 불가능한 선택지들은 제거한다. 그다음 나머지 두 개 중의 하나를 고르고 선택지로 다시 가면 된다.

ADVANCED

1. Linking protection of natural environment to manufacturing firms will assure that the firms. In accordance with this, official documents describing the mechanics of the new policy have been sent by the federal government to all the manufacturing companies in the country. There are two main goals in plan. First, the government wishes to make the companies feel the responsibility of the surrounding environment. Second, through an appropriate reward system, the government encourages the companies to see the environment as one of their assets and to increase economic profits while protecting the environment.

(a) maximize their profits by developing on the protected land

(b) endeavor to successfully keep the natural environment healthy

(c) work with each other to evade the environmental laws

(d) make double profits by protecting the environment

1. Linking protection of natural environment to manufacturing firms will assure that the firms. In accordance with this, official documents describing the mechanics of the new policy have been sent by the federal government to all the manufacturing companies in the country. There are two main goals in plan. First, the government wishes to make the companies feel the responsibility of the surrounding environment. Second, through an appropriate reward system, the government encourages the companies to see the environment as one of their assets and to increase economic profits while protecting the environment.

(a) maximize their profits by developing on the protected land

(b) endeavor to successfully keep the natural environment healthy

(c) work with each other to evade the environmental laws

(d) make double profits by protecting the environment

2. Results from the Statistics Department of the Bank of Korea suggest that _____
_____. First of all, the Gross National Product of Korea has increased
greatly over the past ten years. Furthermore, unemployment rates are down to almost half of
what they used to be. These results reflect the government's constant efforts to bring back what
used to be before the Great Recession of 2008.

(a) the Korean economy is starting to boom

(b) the economy in Korea is always be fluctuating

(c) Korea will face an economic recession

(d) the country should take use of open trade

2. Results from the Statistics Department of the Bank of Korea suggest that _____
_____. First of all, the Gross National Product of Korea has increased
greatly over the past ten years. Furthermore, unemployment rates are down to almost half of
what they used to be. These results reflect the government's constant efforts to bring back what
used to be before the Great Recession of 2008.

(a) the Korean economy is starting to boom

(b) the economy in Korea is always be fluctuating

(c) Korea will face an economic recession

(d) the country should take use of open trade

3. Making a piñata is not as difficult as people might think. First, make paper mache paste by mixing a bowl of flour with water. Second, tear some newspapers into strips. They should be about 2 inches wide and 6 to 8 inches long, making the newspaper to lie nice and flat on the balloon. Next, apply paper mache in a crisscross pattern until the entire balloon is covered. Let the piñata sit until it is completely dried and hardened. After that, pop the balloon and remove it, leaving the mold empty in a balloon-shaped.

Q: What is the passage mainly about?

(a) How to make a sphere-shaped mold

(b) Being careful with handling a balloon

(c) Solution to difficulties of making a piñata with paper mache

(d) Steps necessary for constructing a piñata

3. Making a piñata is not as difficult as people might think. First, make paper mache paste by mixing a bowl of flour with water. Second, tear some newspapers into strips. They should be about 2 inches wide and 6 to 8 inches long, making the newspaper to lie nice and flat on the balloon. Next, apply paper mache in a crisscross pattern until the entire balloon is covered. Let the piñata sit until it is completely dried and hardened. After that, pop the balloon and remove it, leaving the mold empty in a balloon-shaped.

Q: What is the passage mainly about?

(a) How to make a sphere-shaped mold

(b) Being careful with handling a balloon

(c) Solution to difficulties of making a piñata with paper mache

(d) Steps necessary for constructing a piñata

4. The terminology, "Quantum physics" is a branch of science dealing with physical phenomena on a diminutive level. It provides a mathematical description of 'particle-like' and 'wave-like' behavior and interactions of energy and matter. In epitome, one of the main ideas of Quantum Theory states that it is physically impossible to know both the position and the particle's momentum at the same time. Another idea of the theory claims that the atomic world is nothing like the world we live in. While these may sound unfamiliar and strange at a glance, Quantum physics provides clues to the field of science and the fundamental nature of the universe.

Q: What is the main topic of the passage?

(a) The ways in which particles and matters interact with one another

(b) Energy decides the momentum of a particle

(c) An overall explanation on Quantum physics

(d) A description on the scientific theories provided by Quantum

4. The terminology, "Quantum physics" is a branch of science dealing with physical phenomena on a diminutive level. It provides a mathematical description of 'particle-like' and 'wave-like' behavior and interactions of energy and matter. In epitome, one of the main ideas of Quantum Theory states that it is physically impossible to know both the position and the particle's momentum at the same time. Another idea of the theory claims that the atomic world is nothing like the world we live in. While these may sound unfamiliar and strange at a glance, Quantum physics provides clues to the field of science and the fundamental nature of the universe.

Q: What is the main topic of the passage?

(a) The ways in which particles and matters interact with one another

(b) Energy decides the momentum of a particle

(c) An overall explanation on Quantum physics

(d) A description on the scientific theories provided by Quantum

5. _____ is definitely not an ambition that most elementary school teachers would try to accomplish, yet Donna Caterano was a woman of overflowing passion. She voluntarily invested her free time to help blind and deaf children start from a blank slate and gradually develop their academic skills one step at a time. With her teeming desire to support the children, she has succeeded in helping more than 100 blind and deaf elementary students to reach the level of other students in subjects which include but are not limited to writing, math, and science. Furthermore, Donna continued her progress even outside of the elementary school; by helping the disabled elderly who wish to go back to studying academics fulfill their dreams through weekly night classes.

(a) Granting free education for students lacking money

(b) Providing academics for disabled children rather than recreational activities

(c) Implementing math and science night classes for elderly

(d) Helping children with disabilities catch up to normal students in an academic setting

5. _____ is definitely not an ambition that most elementary school teachers would try to accomplish, yet Donna Caterano was a woman of overflowing passion. She voluntarily invested her free time to help blind and deaf children start from a blank slate and gradually develop their academic skills one step at a time. With her teeming desire to support the children, she has succeeded in helping more than 100 blind and deaf elementary students to reach the level of other students in subjects which include but are not limited to writing, math, and science. Furthermore, Donna continued her progress even outside of the elementary school; by helping the disabled elderly who wish to go back to studying academics fulfill their dreams through weekly night classes.

(a) Granting free education for students lacking money

(b) Providing academics for disabled children rather than recreational activities

(c) Implementing math and science night classes for elderly

(d) Helping people with disabilities catch up to normal students in an academic setting

14

꼬리의 꼬리 물기

14 꼬리의 꼬리 물기

이번 단원의 부제는 "역추론"이라고 할 수 있겠다. 일반적인 문제풀이 방법은 "정추론"에 해당이 된다. 앞에서부터 중요도 상관없이 읽기 때문에 "정"추론인 것이다. 하지만 우리는 중요한 부분부터 차례대로 읽는다. 중요한 문장을 읽게 되면 결국 빈칸에서 묻는 것과 일치하는 경우가 90% 이상이다. 나머지 경우에 꼬리의 꼬리물기 기술이 적용되는 것이다.

✳ 쏘아보기 단서

This, These

✳ 원리 설명

This를 번역하면 '이것'이다. 즉, This 라는 단어가 나온다는 것은, 바로 앞 문장에 대한 부연 설명을 한다는 것이다. 앞 문장의 '이것'과 관련된 부연설명이 나열 되는 것이기 때문이다. 즉, THIS가 나온다면 앞 문장과 뒷 문장은 한 문장이라고 간주하면 될 것이고, 앞 문장에 강조점이 간다는 것도 확인해야 한다.

✳ 문제 풀이

쏘아보기 단서들을 기준으로 중요한 문장 두 문장을 찾았다고 하고, 그 문장 중 한 문장이 THIS로 시작한다고 하면, THIS가 등장한 문장 앞 문장에 집중 해야 한다.
예를 들어, For example 앞의 문장이 This로 시작한다면 For example 앞의 앞 문장을 읽어야 한다.

우선 30~40초동안 문제를 먼저 풀어보세요.

1. According to the teachings of Bei Tsu, there is one most important factor that decides the harvest of a certain year. It is the frequency and the amount of annual rainfall. He says that the amount of rainfall throughout a year controls the success of the year's harvest. This is shown by the fact that some areas harvest more crops at the end of the year, even though the fertility of the soil was judged to be similar. For example, ancient records show that two fields with similar fertility and different rainfall had significantly different harvests, whereas two fields with similar rainfall and different fertility did not show much difference in the end. The obvious conclusion Bei Tsu made was that rainfall is _____.

(a) the deciding factor in a year's harvest is in the amount of rainfall

(b) irrelevant to deciding how much crops will be harvested that year

(c) detrimental to the growing of rice crops in some very fertile lands

(d) one of the most important factors which decide the fertility of the soil

1. According to the teachings of Bei Tsu, there is one most important factor that decides the harvest of a certain year. It is the frequency and the amount of annual rainfall. He says that the amount of rainfall throughout a year controls the success of the year's harvest. This is shown by the fact that some areas harvest more crops at the end of the year, even though the fertility of the soil was judged to be similar. For example, ancient records show that two fields with similar fertility and different rainfall had significantly different harvests, whereas two fields with similar rainfall and different fertility did not show much difference in the end. The obvious conclusion Bei Tsu made was that rainfall is _____.

(a) the deciding factor in a year's harvest is in the amount of rainfall

(b) irrelevant to deciding how much crops will be harvested that year

(c) detrimental to the growing of rice crops in some very fertile lands

(d) one of the most important factors which decide the fertility of the soil

2. Liquid-State Drive (LSD) is a newly invented memory storage system adopted in the most cutting edge computer systems of today. A strange thing about this new technology is that high performance computers with high capacity LSDs tend to malfunction when used in space stations. This is because the liquid state of the drive, which normally allows the drive to change flexibly depending on what sector the necessary data is stored in, makes it float around haphazardly around the computer, causing short circuits and memory corruption. The weightless state in space stations were not put into consideration when LSD was first invented. Thus, the weightlessness makes the LSDs original advantages _____ _____.

(a) not as effective as it is back down on Earth

(b) possible to be used for different purposes

(c) offset its disadvantages of its liquid state

(d) become a problem that needs to be solved

2. Liquid-State Drive (LSD) is a newly invented memory storage system adopted in the most cutting edge computer systems of today. A strange thing about this new technology is that high performance computers with high capacity LSDs tend to malfunction when used in space stations. This is because the liquid state of the drive, which normally allows the drive to change flexibly depending on what sector the necessary data is stored in, makes it float around haphazardly around the computer, causing short circuits and memory corruption. The weightless state in space stations were not put into consideration when LSD was first invented. Thus, the weightlessness makes the LSDs original advantages _____ _____.

(a) not as effective as it is back down on Earth

(b) possible to be used for different purposes

(c) offset its disadvantages of its liquid state

(d) become a problem that needs to be solved

3. On December 18, 1992, the thermometers in Svericoldjorn read a record low temperature of -73 degrees Celsius, leaving the power plant and several important electronic equipment out of function, and a large number of people dead due to hypothermia. While the people were stuck in the city, with their cars not starting and heaters not working, the citizens decided to pull down the UNESCO-protected Nordic ruin of Djontsburn, and burn it for fuel. Despite the outrageousness of the idea, this last resort was later accepted and understood worldwide, considering it was the only way to save their lives. From these events, a new provision has been added to the UNESCO cultural heritage regulations, adding that

_____.

(a) a protected cultural heritage site should never be jeopardized

(b) cold regions are henceforth exempt from some of the rules thereof

(c) protection of human life is always a priority to protecting heritage sites

(d) the heritage sites in areas with extreme conditions should be relocated

3. On December 18, 1992, the thermometers in Svericoldjorn read a record low temperature of -73 degrees Celsius, leaving the power plant and several important electronic equipment out of function, and a large number of people dead due to hypothermia. While the people were stuck in the city, with their cars not starting and heaters not working, the citizens decided to pull down the UNESCO-protected Nordic ruin of Djontsburn, and burn it for fuel. Despite the outrageousness of the idea, this last resort was later accepted and understood worldwide, considering it was the only way to save their lives. From these events, a new provision has been added to the UNESCO cultural heritage regulations, adding that

_____.

(a) a protected cultural heritage site should never be jeopardized

(b) cold regions are henceforth exempt from some of the rules thereof

(c) protection of human life is always a priority to protecting heritage sites

(d) the heritage sites in areas with extreme conditions should be relocated

4. Military boot camp is, in a way, a cycle. Newly incoming soldiers enter boot camp every month. Then, they are put into a series of training that will push them to their limits not only physically but mentally and emotionally. But that doesn't mean they don't have a good time because they form bonds with all the people around them. These bonds are very powerful and so a lot of soldiers are motivated to come back to base camp and work as drill officers. Because of this, _____.

(a) forming a sense of camaraderie in the boot camp is the most important.

(b) many trainees become a different person once they leave the camp

(c) there is always an adequate supply of people willing to be a drill officer in boot camp

(d) the number of incoming soldiers increase annually

4. Military boot camp is, in a way, a cycle. Newly incoming soldiers enter boot camp every month. Then, they are put into a series of training that will push them to their limits not only physically but mentally and emotionally. But that doesn't mean they don't have a good time because they form bonds with all the people around them. These bonds are very powerful and so a lot of soldiers are motivated to come back to base camp and work as drill officers. Because of this, _____.

(a) forming a sense of camaraderie in the boot camp is the most important.

(b) many trainees become a different person once they leave the camp

(c) there is always an adequate supply of people willing to be a drill officer in boot camp

(d) the number of incoming soldiers increase annually

5. Immigrant workers are forced to confront critical difficulties regarding insurance problems. As they lack authorized documents, they have no method of being issued insurances in a legal manner. This is especially a major problem in one specific area: health insurance. Visiting the doctor for even simple medical check-ups cost a fortune without the possession of a health insurance, and consequently the illegal immigrants seldom go to the hospital, resulting in frequent illness and constant fatigue. So, an answer to this problem is _____

_____.

(a) to aid workers in the process of receiving medical check-ups

(b) to find a way to get illegal workers to visit the hospital more often

(c) to improve the working conditions of immigrant workers

(d) not to show negative opinions about people lacking health insurances

5. Immigrant workers are forced to confront critical difficulties regarding insurance problems. As they lack authorized documents, they have no method of being issued insurances in a legal manner. This is especially a major problem in one specific area: health insurance. Visiting the doctor for even simple medical check-ups cost a fortune without the possession of a health insurance, and consequently the illegal immigrants seldom go to the hospital, resulting in frequent illness and constant fatigue. So, an answer to this problem is _____

_____.

(a) to aid workers in the process of receiving medical check-ups

(b) to find a way to get illegal workers to visit the hospital more often

(c) to improve the working conditions of immigrant workers

(d) not to show negative opinions about people lacking health insurances

15

인과 관계

15 인과 관계

XX 때문에 YY가 되었다. 라고 하는 인과 구조에서 X가 원인 Y가 결과라는 것을 알 수 있을 것이다. 텝스 시험에서 인과관계가 등장한다면 결과에 초점을 둬야 하는 것이 맞다. 이번 단원에선 인과관계를 나타내는 단서들과 이 단서들이 모여서 이뤄지는 인과관계 유형이 어떤 것인지 살펴본다.

✽ 쏘아보기 단서

✽ 원리 설명

지문의 유형 중 시험 당 한 문제 정도 등장하는 것이 바로 인과 관계 구조의 유형이다. 이 유형의 지문들에는 인과 관계가 여러 번 반복해서 등장한다. 위 그림에서 보다시피 인과가 계속 맞물리게 되면, 마지막 문장이 가장 중요하게 되는 것이다. 일반적인 글 읽기 시 첫 문장부터 차례대로 읽으며 마지막 문장을 이해하게 되겠지만, 쏘아보기를 통해 발견을 한다면 수월하게 문제를 풀 수 있다.

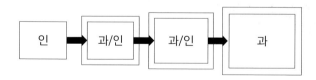

✽ 문제 풀이

- 빈칸이 마지막에 있고

- 마지막 문장이 So, Then, Consequently, As a result 로 시작하고

- ▮▮▮▮▮▮▮▮▮▮▮▮▮▮▮▮▮▮▮▮▮▮▮▮▮▮

지문은 인과관계로 생각하면 된다.

인과관계 유형을 발견 한다면 첫 문장과 뒤에서 두 번째 문장, 그리고 빈칸을 읽으면 문제는 풀린다.

✎

우선 30~40초동안 문제를 먼저 풀어보세요.

1. Modern drug traffickers are constantly inventing many imaginative ways of producing, smuggling and trading drugs, and it seems the current control and surveillance is usually insufficient to counteract them. Since the police department's input of resources into the matter is so small, the police are often too slow to react to new tricks of the trade, which means the drug traffickers are always a step ahead. Consequently, by the time the police find out about a new trick the drug traffickers use, _____.

(a) they are likely to have already moved onto a new one

(b) it is only a matter of time before they are tracked down

(c) they do not have enough men to crack down on them

(d) they shift their efforts to other available lucrative goods

1. Modern drug traffickers are constantly inventing many imaginative ways of producing, smuggling and trading drugs, and it seems the current control and surveillance is usually insufficient to counteract them. Since the police department's input of resources into the matter is so small, the police are often too slow to react to new tricks of the trade, which means the drug traffickers are always a step ahead. Consequently, by the time the police find out about a new trick the drug traffickers use, _____.

(a) they are likely to have already moved onto a new one

(b) it is only a matter of time before they are tracked down

(c) they do not have enough men to crack down on them

(d) they shift their efforts to other available lucrative goods

2. It is very common for people to use poison to eliminate rats and mice in their homes. Just by leaving a few poisoned tablets around the corners of the house, rats, mice and various nuisances are easily gotten rid of without fuss. However, a great many species of rats have already become immune of the chemicals used in typical rat poison. As a result, most mice just fall sick for a week or two then recover, scurrying around behind walls and under the floor once again. Therefore, _____.

(a) the rats and mice do not find the poison a threat

(b) it is not recommended to try to get rid of such vermin

(c) the method is no longer as effective as it used to be

(d) using poison only strengthens the rats and mice

2. It is very common for people to use poison to eliminate rats and mice in their homes. Just by leaving a few poisoned tablets around the corners of the house, rats, mice and various nuisances are easily gotten rid of without fuss. However, a great many species of rats have already become immune of the chemicals used in typical rat poison. As a result, most mice just fall sick for a week or two then recover, scurrying around behind walls and under the floor once again. Therefore, _____.

(a) the rats and mice do not find the poison a threat

(b) it is not recommended to try to get rid of such vermin

(c) the method is no longer as effective as it used to be

(d) using poison only strengthens the rats and mice

3. The city of New York has recently come up with strategies to reduce noise pollution in the streets. There have been various complaints by citizens due to the excessive noise of music, cars and entertainment outside streets. A study revealed that 62% of the citizens have disrupted sleeping patterns due to the loud noise in the city. The city plans to reduce noise pollution by putting a quiet zone from 11:00pm to 2:00am on weekdays. Although many are quite skeptical of this new policy, experts claim that _____.

(a) it is expected to reduce noise pollution

(b) the policy would not have any effect whatsoever

(c) the city noise level should be reduced

(d) citizens should use public transportation instead of cars

3. The city of New York has recently come up with strategies to reduce noise pollution in the streets. There have been various complaints by citizens due to the excessive noise of music, cars and entertainment outside streets. A study revealed that 62% of the citizens have disrupted sleeping patterns due to the loud noise in the city. The city plans to reduce noise pollution by putting a quiet zone from 11:00pm to 2:00am on weekdays. Although many are quite skeptical of this new policy, experts claim that _____.

(a) it is expected to reduce noise pollution

(b) the policy would not have any effect whatsoever

(c) the city noise level should be reduced

(d) citizens should use public transportation instead of cars

4. Immigrant workers are forced to confront critical difficulties regarding insurance problems. As they lack authorized documents, they have no method of being issued insurances in a legal manner. This is especially a major problem in one specific area: health insurance. Visiting the doctor for even simple medical check-ups cost a fortune without the possession of a health insurance, and consequently the illegal immigrants seldom go to the hospital, resulting in frequent illness and constant fatigue. So, an answer to this problem is

_____.

(a) to aid workers in the process of receiving medical check-ups

(b) to make the process of obtaining authorized documents easier for immigrant workers

(c) to improve the working conditions of immigrant workers

(d) not to show negative opinions about people lacking health insurances

4. Immigrant workers are forced to confront critical difficulties regarding insurance problems. As they lack authorized documents, they have no method of being issued insurances in a legal manner. This is especially a major problem in one specific area: health insurance. Visiting the doctor for even simple medical check-ups cost a fortune without the possession of a health insurance, and consequently the illegal immigrants seldom go to the hospital, resulting in frequent illness and constant fatigue. So, an answer to this problem is

_____.

(a) to aid workers in the process of receiving medical check-ups

(b) to make the process of obtaining authorized documents easier for immigrant workers

(c) to improve the working conditions of immigrant workers

(d) not to show negative opinions about people lacking health insurances

5. Since the 1975 labor riots, the Dian'an Region's local textile industry has been in crisis. Initially, the casualties and collateral damage from such a violent uprising caused the production capacity to decrease sharply. Once the region recovered from the shock, a new problem arose for the local industry: overpowered textile labor unions, which have made the industry much less lucrative and less competitive. Consequently, in order to try to reinvigorate the region's signature texture industry, the regional government Premier Yu Xianmei has suggested _____

_____ .

(a) that the labor unions collaborate with the government to further their rights

(b) that the labor laws must be reexamined to prevent unjust labor exploitation

(c) providing government subsidies to textile companies until the issue subsides

(d) that the law be revised to limit the power of the textile labor union

5. Since the 1975 labor riots, the Dian'an Region's local textile industry has been in crisis. Initially, the casualties and collateral damage from such a violent uprising caused the production capacity to decrease sharply. Once the region recovered from the shock, a new problem arose for the local industry: overpowered textile labor unions, which have made the industry much less lucrative and less competitive. Consequently, in order to try to reinvigorate the region's signature texture industry, the regional government Premier Yu Xianmei has suggested _____

_____ .

(a) that the labor unions collaborate with the government to further their rights

(b) that the labor laws must be reexamined to prevent unjust labor exploitation

(c) providing government subsidies to textile companies until the issue subsides

(d) that the law be revised to limit the power of the textile labor union

16 시간 흐름

16 시간 흐름

어떤 대상이 시간이 지남에 따라 변화하는 과정이 나타나는 것을 다루는 단원이다. 특정인물의 성장과정 혹은 사물/현상의 변화 과정을 나타내는 지문들은 모두 동일한 원칙이 있고, 문제풀이에 이 원칙들을 적용해 보면, 정확도가 올라 쉽고 편리하게 문제를 풀 수 있다.

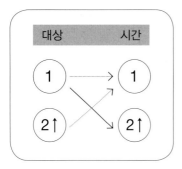

�֎ 쏘아보기 단서

1. ▨▨▨▨▨▨▨▨▨▨▨▨▨▨▨

2. 쏘아보기 단락 (문장 시작 후 2~3 단어 후 쉼표가 나오는 경우)(ex. As time progressed, Later, Afterwards, 등 시간 흐름을 나타내는 단어들)

3. ▨▨▨▨▨▨▨▨▨▨▨▨▨▨▨▨▨ Rise, Growth, 등

�֎ 원리 설명

시간 흐름은 결국 X라는 대상이 A → B → C → D 라는 시간을 지나서 변화하는 것이다. 주제는 "X의 변화과정" 이 되는 것이다. 결국, 주제 파악만 하게 된다면 모든 문제를 풀 수 있다. A단계와 D단계 중에 X의 변화 과정에서 가장 중요한 것은 D일 것이다. 주제를 파악하기 위해서는 D를 파악한다면 문제는 쉽게 풀린다.

www.teps19.com

❋ 문제 풀이

시간 흐름이 충족되려면 시간 흐름 쏘아보기 단서 중에서 ▨▨▨▨▨ 이상이 등장해야, 시간 흐름이 되는 것이다. 시간 흐름 유형에 속하게 되면, 쏘아보기 단서들 중 지문 가장 뒤쪽에 위치한 단서가 들어간 문장을 읽는다. "시간 흐름"이라는 틀 속에 그 문장을 추가한다면 정답은 무조건 나온다.

우선 30~40초동안 문제를 먼저 풀어보세요.

1. In 1985, the National Land Swimming Championships Committee was established as the nation's first land swimming competition host. The first land swimming race, which was held on the Paddington Olympics Stadium, took place soon after the Committee was founded. Five years after this event in 1990, an even bigger land swimming competition was held in Los Angeles, and the sport's popularity reached its pinnacle, far exceeding that of baseball and football. The popular sport took a sharp downturn, however, when it was found in 1992 that the committee was manipulating the game results for monetary gains. As time progressed, the people slowly forgot about the sport, and now very few people remember that such a sport even existed.

Q: What is the passage mainly about?

(a) The dangers of swimming on land without proper equipment

(b) The beginning of a new popular sport which prospered in the 90s

(c) The decline of a popular sport due to accusations of game rigging

(d) The astounding speed in which people can forget about past issues

1. In 1985, the National Land Swimming Championships Committee was established as the nation's first land swimming competition host. The first land swimming race, which was held on the Paddington Olympics Stadium, took place soon after the Committee was founded. Five years after this event in 1990, an even bigger land swimming competition was held in Los Angeles, and the sport's popularity reached its pinnacle, far exceeding that of baseball and football. The popular sport took a sharp downturn, however, when it was found in 1992 that the committee was manipulating the game results for monetary gains. As time progressed, the people slowly forgot about the sport, and now very few people remember that such a sport even existed.

Q: What is the passage mainly about?

(a) The dangers of swimming on land without proper equipment

(b) The beginning of a new popular sport which prospered in the 90s

(c) The decline of a popular sport due to accusations of game rigging

(d) The astounding speed in which people can forget about past issues

2. After several tragic accidents, the public antipathy toward guns has much grown. One of the primary causes of this change was due to a catastrophic gun rampage in a college event last year, which killed 45 and injured hundreds. The increase in the number of minor gun accidents in general has been one of the reasons of the escalating stigma towards guns. Such movements have also been stimulated by the Self-Defense Act that passed congress last month, loosening qualification standards required to carry concealed-carry weapons and made it no longer illegal to hold guns in some public premises like colleges. Also the increased popularity of peace oriented cults also has stimulated this rising tension.

Q: What is the passage mainly about?

(a) Tragic incidents involving shootings which took place last year

(b) The relationships between public consensus and media coverage

(c) Weapon related regulations and its effect on the public's sentiments

(d) Reasons for the growing public autipathy towards guns

2. After several tragic accidents, the public antipathy toward guns has much grown. One of the primary causes of this change was due to a catastrophic gun rampage in a college event last year, which killed 45 and injured hundreds. The increase in the number of minor gun accidents in general has been one of the reasons of the escalating stigma towards guns. Such movements have also been stimulated by the Self-Defense Act that passed congress last month, loosening qualification standards required to carry concealed-carry weapons and made it no longer illegal to hold guns in some public premises like colleges. Also the increased popularity of peace oriented cults also has stimulated this rising tension.

Q: What is the passage mainly about?

(a) Tragic incidents involving shootings which took place last year

(b) The relationships between public consensus and media coverage

(c) Weapon related regulations and its effect on the public's sentiments

(d) Reasons for the growing public autipathy towards guns

3. The National "Cats as Pets" movement has followed along the general trend of popularizing pet animals that became mainstream from 2010 up until now. The videos produced by the partakers of this movement intended to awaken people to the cuteness of cats and to encourage cats as pets. The leaders of this movement used various methods such as Facebook and Twitter to create imaginary anthropomorphic cat personalities which would continually post pictures of its "friends". Although the beginning of this movement is unclear, it is thought to be the popularization of SNS media which allowed it to become easily known to the greater public.

Q: What is the main topic of the passage?

(a) The popularity of cats as pets from around 2010

(b) The beginning of the National Cats as Pets Movement

(c) The importance of cats in the general tendency of the time

(d) The prosperity of cats as imaginary pets through the SNS media

3. The National "Cats as Pets" movement has followed along the general trend of popularizing pet animals that became mainstream from 2010 up until now. The videos produced by the partakers of this movement intended to awaken people to the cuteness of cats and to encourage cats as pets. The leaders of this movement used various methods such as Facebook and Twitter to create imaginary anthropomorphic cat personalities which would continually post pictures of its "friends". Although the beginning of this movement is unclear, it is thought to be the popularization of SNS media which allowed it to become easily known to the greater public.

Q: What is the main topic of the passage?

(a) The popularity of cats as pets from around 2010

(b) The beginning of the National Cats as Pets Movement

(c) The importance of cats in the general tendency of the time

(d) The prosperity of cats as imaginary pets through the SNS media

4. In his 1433 play The Venetian Flea Chaser, Venetian playwright Lorenzo de Vecco, critically portrayed recent history, something that had never been seen in western literature. He addressed many historical controversies, especially those regarding Italian politics, including the notorious corruption in his home city Venice that once undermined the very foundation of Italian commerce. For Lorenzo, the rising prosperity of the western world during the 15th century could not hide the horrible and wasteful incidents that took place in the previous century.

Q: What is the main topic of the passage?

(a) What socio-historical conflicts Lorenzo predicted.

(b) How historical controversies were portrayed in western literature.

(c) How greater prosperity of the western world affected renaissance literature.

(d) How Lorenzo de Vecco depicted history negatively

4. In his 1433 play The Venetian Flea Chaser, Venetian playwright Lorenzo de Vecco, critically portrayed recent history, something that had never been seen in western literature. He addressed many historical controversies, especially those regarding Italian politics, including the notorious corruption in his home city Venice that once undermined the very foundation of Italian commerce. For Lorenzo, the rising prosperity of the western world during the 15th century could not hide the horrible and wasteful incidents that took place in the previous century.

Q: What is the main topic of the passage?

(a) What socio-historical conflicts Lorenzo predicted.

(b) How historical controversies were portrayed in western literature.

(c) How greater prosperity of the western world affected renaissance literature.

(d) How Lorenzo de Vecco depicted history negatively

5. During the 17th century, farmers and peasants normally ate multigrain rice. Since white rice was extremely valuable, the poor used various grains that could be easily obtained in their front yards and mixed them with pure white rice. This helped increase the volume of rice and was crucial in fighting hunger. By the end of the 20th century, however, _____.

(a) multigrain rice had become the modern luxury good

(b) people only ate multigrain rice

(c) wheat replaced rice as the staple food

(d) white rice was no longer available

5. During the 17th century, farmers and peasants normally ate multigrain rice. Since white rice was extremely valuable, the poor used various grains that could be easily obtained in their front yards and mixed them with pure white rice. This helped increase the volume of rice and was crucial in fighting hunger. By the end of the 20th century, however, _____.

(a) multigrain rice had become the modern luxury good

(b) people only ate multigrain rice

(c) wheat replaced rice as the staple food

(d) white rice was no longer available

17

트윈타워

17 트윈타워

지문 내에서 두 개의 개념을 비교 대조하는 식의 글들도 자주 등장한다. 또한, 어떤 사안에 대한 찬성 반대 의견을 나타내는 글들도 많다. 이런 글들을 어떻게 발견하며 발견하게 되면 어떻게 신속히 풀 수 있는지, 그리고 이런 트윈타워 유형의 지문들의 정답들은 어떤 특징을 가졌는지 살펴보아야 한다.

✳ 쏘아보기 단서

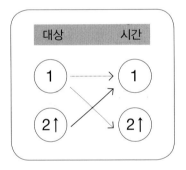

Skepticism, Controversy, Debate, Opponents/Advocates

Both, Neither, Either, Whether,

Two (첫 문장)

✳ 문제 풀이

트윈 타워라는 것을 파악한다면 결국 두 가지의 내용에 대해서 집중하기보단, ▩▩▩▩에 대해서 생각해 봐야 한다. 정확히 A측과 B측이 어떤 이야기를 하고 있는지, 혹은 A와 B는 각각 어떤 의미가 있는지 확인하기 보단, A와 B가 어떤 ▩▩▩▩인지만 파악하려고 노력하면 된다. 트윈 타워 유형의 문제들의 모든 정답은 둘의 ▩▩▩▩에 대한 것이다.

우선 30~40초동안 문제를 먼저 풀어보세요.

1. The Vesuvian Martial Arts routine has been widely assumed to suppress the appetite of an individual performing the art form. After ongoing experiments on the hunger rates of the individuals, researchers at the Ministry of Health in Battanuihi have finally confirmed the norm to be valid. However, what they have not been able to identify is whether the cause for this phenomenon is the uptempo style of movement or the repetitive bobbing motion of the head in the routine. But there also remains a possibility that both factors _____ _____.

(a) will lead the Ministry of Health to find a feasible solution

(b) cause the uptempo movements

(c) are being overlooked in the research

(d) are equally responsible for the decrease in the craving for food

1. The Vesuvian Martial Arts routine has been widely assumed to suppress the appetite of an individual performing the art form. After ongoing experiments on the hunger rates of the individuals, researchers at the Ministry of Health in Battanuihi have finally confirmed the norm to be valid. However, what they have not been able to identify is whether the cause for this phenomenon is the uptempo style of movement or the repetitive bobbing motion of the head in the routine. But there also remains a possibility that both factors _____ _____.

(a) will lead the Ministry of Health to find a feasible solution

(b) cause the uptempo movements

(c) are being overlooked in the research

(d) are equally responsible for the decrease in the craving for food

2. A major debate in understanding language acquisition can be divided into nativist and non-nativist schools. While nativists such as Noam Chomsky focused on hugely complex inborn cognitive abilities, non-nativists accentuated the importance of the environment in which the language is learned. Nativists argue that it is otherwise extremely difficult to explain how children within the first 5 years of life routinely master the complex grammatical rules of their native language. Non-nativists insist that environmental factors influence the way in one thinks, and so cannot be ignored. The division between these two schools is based on whether

_____.

(a) cognitive abilities are developed through nature or nurture

(b) children learn their mother tongue before they become five

(c) Noam Chomsky is right or wrong

(d) language acquisition is due to internal or external factors

2. A major debate in understanding language acquisition can be divided into nativist and non-nativist schools. While nativists such as Noam Chomsky focused on hugely complex inborn cognitive abilities, non-nativists accentuated the importance of the environment in which the language is learned. Nativists argue that it is otherwise extremely difficult to explain how children within the first 5 years of life routinely master the complex grammatical rules of their native language. Non-nativists insist that environmental factors influence the way in one thinks, and so cannot be ignored. The division between these two schools is based on whether

_____.

(a) cognitive abilities are developed through nature or nurture

(b) children learn their mother tongue before they become five

(c) Noam Chomsky is right or wrong

(d) language acquisition is due to internal or external factors

3. People who bank online are always notified beforehand that their transactions online make them liable for fraud. A research conducted on the electronic banking process in Spain has shown that many people with online bank accounts have far less protection against financial fraud than those who bank offline. At the present state, when a credit card is used fraudulently or a check is forged offline, the consumer rarely, if ever, receives the bill and thus the money is usually able to be refunded after an investigation. But this state of affairs _____ _____.

(a) does not apply for purchases conducted online

(b) is likely to be carried out in a similar matter online

(c) might not be considered important in other countries

(d) will be much more precise online

3. People who bank online are always notified beforehand that their transactions online make them liable for fraud. A research conducted on the electronic banking process in Spain has shown that many people with online bank accounts have far less protection against financial fraud than those who bank offline. At the present state, when a credit card is used fraudulently or a check is forged offline, the consumer rarely, if ever, receives the bill and thus the money is usually able to be refunded after an investigation. But this state of affairs _____ _____.

(a) does not apply for purchases conducted online

(b) is likely to be carried out in a similar matter online

(c) might not be considered important in other countries

(d) will be much more precise online

4. Linking protection of natural environment to manufacturing firms will assure that the firms. In accordance with this, official documents describing the mechanics of the new policy have been sent by the federal government to all the manufacturing companies in the country. There are two main goals in plan. First, the government wishes to make the companies feel the responsibility of the surrounding environment. Second, through an appropriate reward system, the government encourages the companies to see the environment as one of their assets and to increase economic profits while protecting the environment.

(a) maximize their profits by developing on the protected land

(b) endeavor to successfully keep the natural environment healthy

(c) work with each other to evade the environmental laws

(d) make double profits by protecting the environment

4. Linking protection of natural environment to manufacturing firms will assure that the firms. In accordance with this, official documents describing the mechanics of the new policy have been sent by the federal government to all the manufacturing companies in the country. There are two main goals in plan. First, the government wishes to make the companies feel the responsibility of the surrounding environment. Second, through an appropriate reward system, the government encourages the companies to see the environment as one of their assets and to increase economic profits while protecting the environment.

(a) maximize their profits by developing on the protected land

(b) endeavor to successfully keep the natural environment healthy

(c) work with each other to evade the environmental laws

(d) make double profits by protecting the environment

5. During the colonial period of America, Puritans, a group of Christians promoting an austere lifestyle, were predominant. Whenever its members would not follow in their footsteps, the Puritan leaders either banished or publically punished them. For example, if an individual was to involve oneself with gluttony-excessive eating and drinking-he or she would be forced to suffer public punishment in the form of a scaffold, which humiliated the offender in front of his or her peers. These types of punishments _____.

(a) led to the early demise of the Puritanism

(b) encouraged rebellious behaviors among citizens

(c) were against the ideals of Puritan leaders

(d) helped sustain a strict Puritan ideology

5. During the colonial period of America, Puritans, a group of Christians promoting an austere lifestyle, were predominant. Whenever its members would not follow in their footsteps, the Puritan leaders either banished or publically punished them. For example, if an individual was to involve oneself with gluttony-excessive eating and drinking-he or she would be forced to suffer public punishment in the form of a scaffold, which humiliated the offender in front of his or her peers. These types of punishments _____.

(a) led to the early demise of the Puritanism

(b) encouraged rebellious behaviors among citizens

(c) were against the ideals of Puritan leaders

(d) helped sustain a strict Puritan ideology

ADVANCED

18

생소개념

18 생소개념

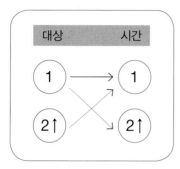

이제까지 대부분의 단원에서 "강조점"을 찾는 것을 목표로 쏘아보기를 해왔을 것이다. 이번 단원에서는 가장 당연한 강조점들이 어디에 있는지 살펴본다. 지문 속의 중요한 대상에 대해 주장이나 강조를 나타내고 있다면 그것이 무조건 주제문이 된다는 원칙에서 출발한다. 문제 대부분에 해당될 수 있는 기술인만큼 쏘아보기 단서들을 꼭 숙지하도록 한다.

✽ 쏘아보기 단서

Allow, Resemble, Realize, Find, Which (is), Believes, Thinks, Supports, Says, Is

Must, Should, Had better, Be to, Have got to, Need to, Insist, Suggest, Recommend, Demand, Pay attention to

It is right (natural, necessary, time) that

✽ 원리 설명

새로운 지문에서 소개하는 개념들은 모두 생소개념이라고 정의한다.

지문이 "김치"에 대한 설명을 하고 있다면, "김치"를 생소개념으로 정의하는 것이다.

김치가 우리에게 생소한 것은 아니지만, 지문이 중점적으로 설명하고 있는 대상이라면, 생소개념이 되는 것이다.

이 생소개념은 지문 내에서 여러 번 등장하게 된다. 그리고 그 중 한번이 주제문이 되는 것이다. 기존 문제 풀이 방식으로는 다 읽기 전까지 주제문을 알 수 없었지만, 이젠 생소개념 뒤에 나오는 동사들에 집중하면 수월하게 풀 수 있다.

✳ 문제 풀이

쏘아보기 혹은 첫 문장을 읽는 단계에서 생소개념을 발견하게 된다면 지문 내에 등장하는 생소개념 뒤의 동사에 집중한다.

그 중 쏘아보기 단서에 나오는 단서들이 등장한다면, 그 문장이 주제문이 되는 것이다.

웬만한 지문엔 생소개념 뒤에 단서는 단 한 번만 등장하고, 2개가 등장한다면 그 2문장을 함께 읽고 문제를 풀면 된다.

1. A recent investigation revealed that the material buried in the cryotic soil, also known as permafrost, is _____. The main object of this excavation was to subsequently revitalize the already extinct Mammuthus primigenius from approximately 12,000 years ago using the tissue frozen in the permafrost. The samples ejected from the cryotic soil were then investigated by the researchers of Sooam Biotech Research Foundation to confirm that the cells were compatible. The results of the study affirmed that an adequate nucleus was found to potentially hold DNA to create a blastocyst implantable to a surrogate mother. This recent investigation hinted at a possibility of mankind being able to bid defiance to the laws of nature.

(a) slowly melting due to global warming

(b) crucial in studying the DNA of the surrogate mother

(c) a starting point to proving human's ability to reverse time

(d) evidence of life existing 12,000 years ago

1. A recent investigation revealed that the material buried in the cryotic soil, also known as permafrost, is _____. The main object of this excavation was to subsequently revitalize the already extinct Mammuthus primigenius from approximately 12,000 years ago using the tissue frozen in the permafrost. The samples ejected from the cryotic soil were then investigated by the researchers of Sooam Biotech Research Foundation to confirm that the cells were compatible. The results of the study affirmed that an adequate nucleus was found to potentially hold DNA to create a blastocyst implantable to a surrogate mother. This recent investigation hinted at a possibility of mankind being able to bid defiance to the laws of nature.

(a) slowly melting due to global warming

(b) crucial in studying the DNA of the surrogate mother

(c) a starting point to proving human's ability to reverse time

(d) evidence of life existing 12,000 years ago

2. Herpes simplex virus accesses human cells, homes on the nucleus and then directs itself into the DNA using high pressure stimulated from a nanometer-scale protein shell known as the capsidpropel. This virus is known to cause infections such as influenza and HIV. However, the Herpes simplex virus is becoming resistant to medicines that aim at the viral proteins, which can instantaneously convert themselves and develop resistance to anti-viral drugs due to genetic mutation. Scientists, thus, are hoping to create a potent drug to reduce the resistance level. So far, they have experimented on mice to create an adequate drug. This could help

_____.

(a) detect the reason behind the genetic mutation

(b) keep the virus from seeking other viral proteins

(c) develop a new treatment to attack the influenza

(d) prevent the virus from remaining resistant to the drug

2. Herpes simplex virus accesses human cells, homes on the nucleus and then directs itself into the DNA using high pressure stimulated from a nanometer-scale protein shell known as the capsidpropel. This virus is known to cause infections such as influenza and HIV. However, the Herpes simplex virus is becoming resistant to medicines that aim at the viral proteins, which can instantaneously convert themselves and develop resistance to anti-viral drugs due to genetic mutation. Scientists, thus, are hoping to create a potent drug to reduce the resistance level. So far, they have experimented on mice to create an adequate drug. This could help

_____.

(a) detect the reason behind the genetic mutation

(b) keep the virus from seeking other viral proteins

(c) develop a new treatment to attack the influenza

(d) prevent the virus from remaining resistant to the drug

3. James the Vicious, who ruled Eastern India from 1540 to 1600, is the most feared king in the country's history. A man born from a poor slave family, he came to the throne through a coup-de-tat. He incessantly waged wars against adjacent nations, enjoyed brutal battles between his slaves, conscripted men as his personal body guards and robbed parents of their daughters for his pleasure. Due to such cruel deeds, he is _____.

(a) venerated as an audacious and strong soldier

(b) sentenced to serve maximum penalty in prison

(c) known as the most effective ruler of the century

(d) considered to be the most notorious king

3. James the Vicious, who ruled Eastern India from 1540 to 1600, is the most feared king in the country's history. A man born from a poor slave family, he came to the throne through a coup-de-tat. He incessantly waged wars against adjacent nations, enjoyed brutal battles between his slaves, conscripted men as his personal body guards and robbed parents of their daughters for his pleasure. Due to such cruel deeds, he is _____.

(a) venerated as an audacious and strong soldier

(b) sentenced to serve maximum penalty in prison

(c) known as the most effective ruler of the century

(d) considered to be the most notorious king

4. During the early 19th century, a style of painting called "Impressionism" emerged from the French art, which had previously been largely academic. It was associated most often with few prominent artists, among whom were Eduard Manet, Claude Monet, and Pierre-Auguste Renoir. The new impressionist art rejected classicism and the French academism. It had a liberal style which would be painted "as it is seen", employing a technique called "en plein air" or "in the open air" hinting the Impressionist tradition of painting casual subjects out in the open. The Impressionist movement significantly influenced the later flow of art, and is noted by some art historians to be the beginning of modern art.

Q: What is the main topic of the passage?

(a) The beginnings of modernism in art

(b) A brief account of the French Impressionist movement

(c) The artists who are most often mentioned in Impressionist art

(b) The influence of French Academism on the French Impressionists

4. During the early 19th century, a style of painting called "Impressionism" emerged from the French art, which had previously been largely academic. It was associated most often with few prominent artists, among whom were Eduard Manet, Claude Monet, and Pierre-Auguste Renoir. The new impressionist art rejected classicism and the French academism. It had a liberal style which would be painted "as it is seen", employing a technique called "en plein air" or "in the open air" hinting the Impressionist tradition of painting casual subjects out in the open. The Impressionist movement significantly influenced the later flow of art, and is noted by some art historians to be the beginning of modern art.

Q: What is the main topic of the passage?

(a) The beginnings of modernism in art

(b) A brief account of the French Impressionist movement

(c) The artists who are most often mentioned in Impressionist art

(b) The influence of French Academism on the French Impressionists

5. Psychodrama is commonly used as a method of therapy in which clients gain insight into their lives. The most basic form of psychodrama originates from the belief that the best way for individuals to give creative responses is by undergoing spontaneous action, which is also known as the theory of "spontaneity-creativity". Researchers have found that when an individual bases one's behaviors on impulse, they are able to acquire new solutions to complicated problems in their lives. Furthermore, the more diverse these spontaneous actions are, the more people are able to deeply understand various circumstances throughout their lives. In short, spontaneity-creativity _____.

(a) connects mundane everyday actions to physical therapy
(b) plays a crucial role in making diversity within clients
(c) describes a theory relating instinctive behavior to problem solving
(d) gives therapist a chance to control innovative ideas given by the clients

5. Psychodrama is commonly used as a method of therapy in which clients gain insight into their lives. The most basic form of psychodrama originates from the belief that the best way for individuals to give creative responses is by undergoing spontaneous action, which is also known as the theory of "spontaneity-creativity". Researchers have found that when an individual bases one's behaviors on impulse, they are able to acquire new solutions to complicated problems in their lives. Furthermore, the more diverse these spontaneous actions are, the more people are able to deeply understand various circumstances throughout their lives. In short, spontaneity-creativity _____.

(a) connects mundane everyday actions to physical therapy
(b) plays a crucial role in making diversity within clients
(c) describes a theory relating instinctive behavior to problem solving
(d) gives therapist a chance to control innovative ideas given by the clients

ADVANCED

STRATEGIC
TEPS

III 선택지공략법

19. 선택지 전략

19 선택지

19 선택지

선택지를 접근 할 때에 확실하게 해야 하는 부분이 있다.

시험에서 선택지가 문제가 되는 것은 선택지 4개 중에 2개가 남았을 때 일 것이다.

선택지 2개가 남았을 때 어떻게 정답을 고를지 그 기준을 모르겠고, 선택지 2개가 남았을 때 고민하는 시간이 오히려 길어진 경험을 했을 것이다.

19단원은 결국 선택지가 두 개 남았을 때 어떻게 최단 기간 내에 가장 정확하게 둘을 비교할지에 대한 부분이다.

대부분 사람들은 선택지가 두 개 (a, c) 남는다면 a를 한번 읽어보고 c를 한번 읽어본다. 그다음 둘 중에서 고민을 하면서 a에 관련해서 맞는지 틀린 지 확인하기 위해 지문으로 올라가서 여기 저기 읽는다. 그래도 모르겠으면 시간 압박도 있으니 c를 한번 읽어보고 지문으로 올라가서 c가 맞는지 파악하려고 한다.

결국 그렇게 하는 것은 애초에 선택지 네 개를 읽어 내려가며 a와 c가 남겨진 상태인 시점에 지문에 대한 이해도와 별반 다를 바 없는 것이고, 결국 정답을 맞힐 확률도 높아지지 않는다. 뿐더러, 지문을 여러 번 반복적으로 읽게 되므로 결국 엄청난 시간을 투자하게 된다. 이러한 접근은 잘못 된 것이다.

결국, 선택지가 두 개 남았을 때엔 접근법이 바뀌어야 한다.

(만약 선택지a와 선택지c 사이에서 고민 중이라면,)

1. a와c를 꼼꼼히 읽는다.

2. a와c의 차이점이 무엇인지 찾아낸다.

3. a와c의 차이점을 각각 키워드 하나로 표현한다.

4. 키워드를 가지고 지문에 올라가서 검증한다.

1~4 순서대로 진행을 한다면 결국 훨씬 수월하게 문제를 접근 할 수 있을 것이다.

고민하는 시간도 줄어들 것이고, 정확도는 완벽에 가까워질 것이다.

www.teps19.com

STRATEGIC
TEPS

IV 체화과정

기존 문제 리뷰
및
총정리

빈
칸
채
우
기

1. Looking for _____? You should come to see the Boston Celtics play at the TD Garden located in downtown Boston! Ticket prices range from 50 dollars to 3000 dollars. Every seat is provided with an adequate amount of beer for you and snacks for you and your kids. The exciting atmosphere will be a great experience for the kids and you will be able to blow off some steam. Visit www.tdgarden.co.kr for more information.

(a) an exciting experience for you and your kids

(b) something to do on the weekend

(c) a place to eat beer and watch basketball

(d) a nice treat for your wife

2. With turnitin. com _____. We digitalize the classroom so that the students can submit their assignments through the internet and also get feedback in a fast and efficient manner. We also provide a state of the art plagiarism prevention system: providing the exact percentage of how much a certain paper matches the words of others. With this system, professors and teachers can have a much easier time picking out the dishonest students in the classroom.

(a) students can have fun learning

(b) teachers have a more important role than before

(c) virtual schools can replace actual schools

(d) education from the teaching perspective becomes efficient

3. British scientists from the University of Oxford and Cambridge has come to the conclusion that Branch Chain Amino Acids, a supplement often used by bodybuilders for faster muscle growth and recovery, _____. 100 athletes all around England were given BCAAs in the form of pills and their muscle growth was measured over a period of one year. However, the results showed no difference from the muscle growth of the control group which received no such supplements.

(a) can cause liver disease

(b) decrease muscle mass

(c) do not live up to its description

(d) are only effective on women

4. Prior to 1879, when the light bulb was invented by the famous Thomas Edison, activities that might seem ordinary to us were practically impossible to perform at night. With the great modern marvel, the light bulb, which provided much needed light in the darkness of night, people were able to go out for dinner, sleep at a later period, and enjoy other leisure activities that were previously impossible. People were enthralled at the fact that light bulbs

_____.

(a) allowed daily routines to be performed at nighttime

(b) could be modified to the more effective fluorescent bulbs

(c) could finally enhance the quality of movies

(d) were released at cheap prices

5. Tobacco Gum was prevalent in Major League Baseball in the United States during the mid to late 20th century, even though it _____. As people were finding out that these tobacco products could lead to cancer, and when the children, after seeing their favorite players use chewing tobacco, were trying them out, Major League officials started banning the use of these products. The players, in the end, chose bubble gum, which was both healthier and more visually appealing.

(a) was mainly consumed in Europe

(b) caused no health hazards for the players

(c) contained many carcinogenic substances

(d) was against the will of the fans

6. During the colonial period of America, Puritans, a group of Christians promoting an austere lifestyle, were predominant. Whenever its members would not follow in their footsteps, the Puritan leaders either banished or publically punished them. For example, if an individual was to involve oneself with gluttony-excessive eating and drinking-he or she would be forced to suffer public punishment in the form of a scaffold, which humiliated the offender in front of his or her peers. These types of punishments _____.

(a) led to the early demise of the Puritanism

(b) encouraged rebellious behaviors among citizens

(c) were against the ideals of Puritan leaders

(d) helped sustain a strict Puritan ideology

7. During the Great Depression in the 1920s, the United States was actually _____
_____. As the economy was under drastic conditions, people were sincerely
wishing to divert their attention from the disastrous situation to more entertainment and
excitement. Thus, classic films including Frankenstein and Gone with the Wind had made their
debuts and received great affection from the public during this time.

(a) turning its attention to films

(b) going under a change particularly in the theater industry

(c) going through major progress economically

(d) globally emerged as a trendsetter in cultural aspects

8. Joanna Carroll has just published a novel that _____.
This book completely reveals the malicious torture tactics that were used upon the women who
had been suspected of being witches and being related to witchcraft. Women of the 17th century
who were charged of witchcraft were forced to suffer from humiliation and excruciating pain of
burning or ripping of the skin. The book's depiction of such preposterous behavior is extremely
graphic, enabling the readers to almost feel the pain from the torture.

(a) vividly sheds light on ludicrous behaviors conducted during witch trials

(b) somehow justifies the conducts of torture during the 17th century

(c) gives attention to different types of torture present in history

(d) tries to understand the underlying meaning of the charges of witchcraft

9. Dear Ms. Clementz,

The University of St. Glenzow _____. We wish to inform you that your application was exceptional, and therefore will be accepting you to our exchange student program. Please send us your student visa and the confirmation application from your school. If you require more information, or wish to change your plans for the exchange program, email us via our university website st.glenzow@edu.org

(a) is excited to invite you to its annual summer camp

(b) would like to welcome you to a new semester

(c) wants to hear more from you

(d) will be recruiting new professors

10. Linking protection of natural environment to manufacturing firms will assure that the firms _____. In accordance with this, official documents describing the mechanics of the new policy have been sent by the federal government to all the manufacturing companies in the country. There are two main goals in plan. First, the government wishes to make the companies feel the responsibility of the surrounding environment. Second, through an appropriate reward system, the government encourages the companies to see the environment as one of their assets and to increase economic profits while protecting the environment.

(a) maximize their profits by developing on the protected land.

(b) endeavor to successfully keep the natural environment healthy.

(c) work with each other to evade the environmental laws.

(d) make double profits by protecting the environment.

11. _____ is utterly natural for most scientists now and then, but it was not a concern for Marie Curie and her husband. Soon after Marie Curie finally succeeded in creating the decigram of pure radium, the treatment to cancer using this matter was newly discovered. A boom of industries using radium exhilarated the price of Curie's finding.

However, she and her husband published the process on extracting radium for the public quoting that the radium belonged to the people. Her insistence on free accessibility to radium brought about developments in creating cures to cancer.

(a) Funding research for adequate experiments

(b) Requesting for intellectual rights for monetary reasons

(c) Patenting scientific discoveries

(d) Delivering the results through publications

12. The city of New York has recently come up with strategies to reduce noise pollution in the streets. There have been various complaints by citizens due to the excessive noise of music, cars and entertainment outside streets. A study revealed that 62% of the citizens have disrupted sleeping patterns due to the loud noise in the city. The city plans to reduce noise pollution by putting a quiet zone from 11:00pm to 2:00am on weekdays. Although many are quite skeptical of this new policy, experts claim that _____.

(a) it is expected to reduce noise pollution

(b) the policy would not have any effect whatsoever

(c) the city noise level should be reduced

(d) citizens should use public transportation instead of cars

13. Don't you think it would be fascinating to _____?
In fact, this is actually possible if you visit our website, freetrips.org. Starting today, we will post information that would require customer opinion about travel journeys: just take 2 minutes to fill out the form, and you will be given 2 free tickets to Hawaii! Make your wish come true by visiting our website. This is your ultimate opportunity to gain an experience that you would never be able to have elsewhere.

(a) play games all day

(b) go on a special vacation for free

(c) share your hobby online

(d) study abroad

14. When consumers go to grocery stores to buy their beef for a family dinner, they may be upset that the price of the beef is too high. At the same time, when farmers bring beef to the market they wish that price of the beef was even higher. These views are not surprising: buyers always want to pay less, but sellers _____. Could a "right price" exist for beef from the standpoint of society as a whole?

(a) want more beef

(b) want less beef

(c) always want to be paid more

(d) always want to be paid less

15. _____ has not been confirmed by anyone. A number of people, however, claim that they started in the early 20th century, when an ice cream stand owner in Coney Island, New York, was selling ice cream at the State Fair. Around noon, when the sun was scorching hot, he ran out of paper cups to serve his ice cream. Not knowing what to do, the ice cream salesman went next door to a waffle salesman and asked him to make cups made of waffles. The ice cream salesman started serving his ice cream in the new cup, and surprisingly, people fell in love with the new "Waffle Cone," and therefore, a new way of serving ice cream was invented.

(a) Why Waffle Cones taste so delicious

(b) Why paper cups were so ineffective

(c) How Waffle Cones came into existence

(d) The negative effects of Waffle Cones

16. Immigrant workers are forced to confront critical difficulties regarding insurance problems. As they lack authorized documents, they have no method of being issued insurances in a legal manner. This is especially a major problem in one specific area: health insurance. Visiting the doctor for even simple medical check-ups cost a fortune without the possession of a health insurance, and consequently the illegal immigrants seldom go to the hospital, resulting in frequent illness and constant fatigue. So, an answer to this problem is _____ _____ .

(a) to aid workers in the process of receiving medical check-ups

(b) to make the process of obtaining authorized documents easier for immigrant workers

(c) to improve the working conditions of immigrant workers

(d) not to show negative opinions about people lacking health insurances

17. With the city of Seoul trying to reduce toxic water, oysters just might be the answer. Studies conducted by the University of Oxford show that oysters breathe in toxic water and let out relatively cleaner water in whatever environment they are in. Inserting 500 oysters into a body of water the size of Lake Eerie will decrease the toxic level by 4.7% in a time span of three weeks. Experts claim that this is the best way to _____.

(a) deal with Seoul's water pollution and toxic waste-

(b) drive up the toxic level in Seoul.

(c) make Lake Eerie clean once and for all.

(d) create a safe ecosystem for oysters.

18. Military boot camp is, in a way, a cycle. Newly incoming soldiers enter boot camp every month. Then, they are put into a series of training that will push them to their limits not only physically but mentally and emotionally. But that doesn't mean they don't have a good time because they form bonds with all the people around them. These bonds are very powerful and so a lot of soldiers are motivated to come back to base camp and work as drill officers. Because of this, _____.

(a) forming a sense of camaraderie in the boot camp is the most important.

(b) many trainees become a different person once they leave the camp

(c) there is always an adequate supply of people willing to be a drill officer in boot camp

(d) the number of incoming soldiers increase annually

19. Korean high schools have only themselves to blame if they find that their students are not attentive during the morning. Most competitive high schools in Korea require students to come to school by 7:40 in the morning. To come to school by this time, students usually need to wake up at six or even earlier. Most studies conducted by psychologists and sleep experts claim that our brain is not fully awake and active by this time. Therefore a better strategy would be to _____.

(a) change the schools into night schools

(b) provide more take home assignments

(c) wake up earlier than six o' clock

(d) start school at a later time

20. Excessive intake of alcohol is very harmful to the human body and can even be lethal in extreme cases. Alcohol in large doses can severely impair vital internal organs such as the liver or the heart. In the pancreas, alcohol causes the production of toxic substances that can lead to pancreatitis, a critical inflammation of blood vessels that prevents proper digestion.
There have been, however, studies that suggest moderate consumption of alcohol can be healthy. Small doses of red wine, for instance, _____.

(a) can be a contributing factor to heart failures

(b) may protect healthy adults from developing coronary heart disease

(c) have been found to increase the risk of developing certain cancers.

(d) may release red toxins into the bloodstream

21. Many teenagers who are into building muscle want to take supplements. These include protein shakes, BCAAs, multi-vitamins, fish oil and etc. All these are dedicated to help building muscle faster and to provide more energy for workouts. Or so they say. There are plenty of evidence and studies that show these supplements to be useless. So it is no wonder that parents are _____.

(a) working out at a less efficient rate than their children.

(b) joining their kids in purchasing these products.

(c) hesitant when it comes to buying these products for their children

(d) concerned about health issues from consuming supplements

22. Results from the Statistics Department of the Bank of Korea suggest that _____ _____. First of all, the Gross National Product of Korea has increased greatly over the past ten years. Furthermore, unemployment rates are down to almost half of what they used to be. These results reflect the government's constant efforts to bring back what used to be before the Great Recession of 2008.

(a) the Korean economy is starting to boom

(b) the economy in Korea is always be fluctuating

(c) Korea will face an economic recession

(d) the country should take use of open trade

23. _____ is definitely not an ambition that most elementary school teachers would try to accomplish, yet Donna Caterano was a woman of overflowing passion. She voluntarily invested her free time to help blind and deaf children start from a blank slate and gradually develop their academic skills one step at a time. With her teeming desire to support the children, she has succeeded in helping more than 100 blind and deaf elementary students to reach the level of other students in subjects which include but are not limited to writing, math, and science. Furthermore, Donna continued her progress even outside of the elementary school; by helping the disabled elderly who wish to go back to studying academics fulfill their dreams through weekly night classes.

(a) Granting free education for students lacking money

(b) Providing academics for disabled children rather than recreational activities

(c) Implementing math and science night classes for elderly

(d) Helping children with disabilities catch up to normal students in an academic setting

24. Although it may seem difficult to sleep when you suffer from insomnia, _____ _____. Various simple measures will help you. For instance, try counting sheep, or drink a cup of warm milk before you lie down. Think about complex mathematical equations that would make your brain fried. If it still doesn't work, take a thick academic book and read it for about 5 minutes. You would find your eyelids slowly getting heavier.

(a) you should find a comfortable bed to help you sleep

(b) there are ways to make falling asleep easier

(c) you should always be more active during the day

(d) sufficient rest is important for a healthy body

25. Recently an energy drink called the "Energy Bottle" has been on sale in local malls. Containing the ingredient Glyzerintine, the drink is known to keep a person awake for 26 hours. For students and businessmen who have limited amount of time and an intensive amount of workload, it may seem efficient to boost up work productivity by consuming the drink. Nevertheless, the World Health Organization recently published a research report claiming that Glyzerintine is toxic, and may increase the risk of heart disease. Therefore taking this into account, people _____.

(a) should be more cautious of having the energy drink

(b) should not stay up for 26 hours

(c) are advised to drink coffee instead

(d) should study the benefits of "Energy Bottle"

26. Statistics provided by UN Development Program reveal that while the United States has always been a capitalist country, the _____. Over several decades, the situation exacerbated. By 2007, the average after-tax income of the top 1 percent had reached $1.3 million, but that of the bottom 20 percent amounted to only $17,800. The richest 20 percent earns in total after tax more than the bottom 80 percent combined. These outcomes challenge the general perception we have of the United States as the "Land of Equal Opportunity".

(a) everyone receives equal opportunity

(b) extent of inequality in society actually expanded

(c) Democratic notions of peace were settled deeply in society

(d) Country was reluctant in caring about the environment

27. During the 17th century, farmers and peasants normally ate multigrain rice. Since white rice was extremely valuable, the poor used various grains that could be easily obtained in their front yards and mixed them with pure white rice. This helped increase the volume of rice and was crucial in fighting hunger. By the end of the 20th century, however, _____ _____.

(a) multigrain rice had become the modern luxury good

(b) people only ate multigrain rice

(c) wheat replaced rice as the staple food

(d) white rice was no longer available

28. The human rights committee is in agreement to the liberation of political prisoners from China during the 1950s. Continuing to hold the politicians captive, who were forcefully arrested without a fair trial, only diminishes the significance of human rights and exudes a notorious reputation among the international society. On the other hand, discharging these prisoners may prompt wreckage in social order. Maintaining strong governmental control will become even harder. However, the committee remains firm that the state should _____ _____.

(a) proceed with the movement to free political prisoners

(b) allow the argument between the government and civilians

(c) reward participants in undertaking the human rights plan

(d) substantially decrease governmental power

29. Herpes simplex virus accesses human cells, homes on the nucleus and then directs itself into the DNA using high pressure stimulated from a nanometer-scale protein shell known as the capsidpropel. This virus is known to cause infections such as influenza and HIV.

However, the Herpes simplex virus is becoming resistant to medicines that aim at the viral proteins, which can instantaneously convert themselves and develop resistance to anti-viral drugs due to genetic mutation. Scientists, thus, are hoping to create a potent drug to reduce the resistance level. So far, they have experimented on mice to create an adequate drug.

This could help _____.

(a) detect the reason behind the genetic mutation

(b) keep the virus from seeking other viral proteins

(c) develop a new treatment to attack the influenza

(d) prevent the virus from remaining resistant to the drug

30. In the book the Last Lecture, Randy Pausch_____.
Randy is a professor at Carnegie Mellon and is diagnosed with pancreatic cancer, which only gives him 3 to 6 months to live. He gradually starts the process of letting go of the little and irrelevant things in life such as fighting with his wife over who does the laundry or worrying about the stains on his car. He, thus, realizes how important spending time with family and friends is and how meaningless and time-consuming some of his previous jobs had been.

(a) explains how cancer influenced his family

(b) realizes the value of time in one's life

(c) bemoans being cursed with pancreatic cancer

(d) rediscovers his love for life

31. The head coach of the 2010 Korean speed skating national team, Leonardo Kim, has long been praised for his _____. Even though he spent most of his skating career on the Korean national team where he earned three gold medals, it was his agility and creative skating skills that considerably influenced the world of speed skating. For instance, in the 1998 Olympic Games, Leonardo first disclosed his cross-legging skating style which is still the fastest known way to skate in a corner and is used by all skaters in speed skating.

(a) outstanding contributions to the development of speed skating

(b) medals for victories during the 1998 Olympic Games.

(c) construction of the Korean Olympics ice rink stadium.

(d) coaching skills he showed after his retirement as a professional.

32. James the Vicious, who ruled Eastern India from 1540 to 1600, is the most feared king in the country's history. A man born from a poor slave family, he came to the throne through a coup-de-tat. He incessantly waged wars against adjacent nations, enjoyed brutal battles between his slaves, conscripted men as his personal body guards and robbed parents of their daughters for his pleasure. Due to such cruel deeds, he is _____.

(a) venerated as an audacious and strong soldier

(b) sentenced to serve maximum penalty in prison

(c) known as the most effective ruler of the century

(d) considered to be the most notorious king

33. Dear Andy,

I am writing to update you on the admission process for the last spot at Benjamin Franklin Academy. So far, the number of candidates remaining has been reduced to three. The academic qualities of you and the other two candidates are outstanding and would be more than befitting for the school. As the number of students that can be admitted is very limited, we unfortunately will be selecting only one candidate. Regardless of the result, please remember that all of you are _____. The finalized decision will be announced next Monday.

Regards,

Justin Blake

Admission Administrator, Benjamin Franklin Academy

(a) students whose schools are going to miss

(b) very likely to become the dearest members of our faculty

(c) wonderful candidates who will be accepted with scholarships

(d) exceptional applicants who would be valuable additions to the school

34. A recent investigation revealed that the material buried in the cryotic soil, also known as permafrost, is _____. The main object of this excavation was to subsequently revitalize the already extinct Mammuthus primigenius from approximately 12,000 years ago using the tissue frozen in the permafrost. The samples ejected from the cryotic soil were then investigated by the researchers of Sooam Biotech Research Foundation to confirm that the cells were compatible. The results of the study affirmed that an adequate nucleus was found to potentially hold DNA to create a blastocyst implantable to a surrogate mother. This recent investigation hinted at a possibility of mankind being able to bid defiance to the laws of nature.

(a) slowly melting due to global warming

(b) crucial in studying the DNA of the surrogate mother

(c) a starting point to proving human's ability to reverse time

(d) evidence of life existing 12,000 years ago

35. When one tries to hatch a baby chick at home, using a Styrofoam box can be an effective solution. However, individuals should still keep in mind that Styrofoam boxes are not the same as ordinary cardboard boxes, and so should be avoided during certain hours. This is because Styrofoam boxes impede the proper flow of air. The inside of the box gets heated during the morning hours, which might negatively influence the egg condition for hatching. Therefore, the Styrofoam box should _____.

(a) be used at night when the temperature is relatively low

(b) determine the optimal temperature of the day

(c) be used at all times when hatching a baby chick at home

(d) be cut into pieces of equal size

36. Psychodrama is commonly used as a method of therapy in which clients gain insight into their lives. The most basic idea form of psychodrama originates from the belief that the best way for individuals to give creative responses is by undergoing spontaneous action, which is also known as the theory of "spontaneity-creativity". Researchers have found that when an individual bases one's behaviors on impulse, they are able to acquire new solutions to complicated problems in their lives. Furthermore, the more diverse these spontaneous actions are, the more people are able to deeply understand various circumstances throughout their lives. In short, spontaneity-creativity _____.

(a) connects mundane everyday actions to physical therapy

(b) plays a crucial role in making diversity within clients

(c) describes a theory relating instinctive behavior to problem solving

(d) gives therapist a chance to control innovative ideas given by the clients

37. During the decline of Köln Freistadt, the city officials mainly concentrated on law enforcement instead of reviving the city's withering commerce. It was their belief that restoring public order would help the city regain its former prosperity and effectively counter the impending collapse. However, the resulting harsh surveillance and restrictions only caused the city's economy to stagnate even further, since many merchants and craftsmen saw a sharp decrease in floating population, and thus, less profit. Moreover, corruption was rampant among the overly empowered police force, eating away even more of the city's commercial vigor. Therefore, _____ only accelerated the demise of Köln Freistadt.

(a) the commercial inactivity of the merchants and craftsmen

(b) the restoration of public order that put the city back on track

(c) the public order policies imposed to revitalize the city

(d) the corruption of the law enforcement civil workers

38. It is only recently that people started eating broccoli as food. In fact, the cap of the plant was historically a natural scrub with which the medieval peasants cleaned their latrines. It is very common for archaeologists to come across broccoli residue in medieval ruins, very often together with fecal matter. Their image as a sanitary device was so well recognized among the peasants that no one dared to try eating it. Similarly, _____ _____. A 1304 court document in Köln Freistadt describing broccoli chose words like vile, filthy and cursed, indicating even the aristocrats had an aversion for broccoli. Even though the aristocrats did not use broccoli for sanitary purposes, it seems that its peculiar taste was shunned by people of all classes, no doubt never being considered for food.

(a) a very negative image of broccoli prevailed among the aristocrats

(b) other organic materials like sea sponge was used for sanitary purposes

(c) aristocrats did have some different thoughts about broccoli and its tastes

(d) broccoli began to be considered somewhat edible from the 14th century onwards.

39. Many people, when they picture the Tasty Mango Islands, they think of an island country full of romance and breathtaking scenery. However, this is quite contrary to reality. The island has been dealing with an extreme overpopulation crisis since it was first established. In fact, the problem has penetrated the island to such an extent that it has become acceptable and even recommended to walk on people's shoulders when one becomes immobilized in an overcrowded place. The Tasty Mango Island government has been coming up with various measures to fight the problem, but so far none of them has effectively alleviated the problem. The truth is, the island is a stifling pack of tourists and residents with nothing but people's head to see.

Q. What is the main topic of the passage?

(a) The Tasty Mango Island government's policies to counter the overpopulation

(b) The reality of Tasty Mango Islands contrasted to a common misconception

(c) Reasons that the Tasty Mango Islands is no longer what people used to know

(d) Customs that the Island residents have developed adapting to their environment

40. Iberian Stone Axes of the Paleolithic were made by chipping and cracking rocks by whatever means possible, until the desired shape was achieved. However, a closer inspection reveals that, despite the crude crafting method, the craftsmen who made these axes were masterfully in control of their methods. Just about all of them found within one region seems to share surprisingly identical shapes, suggesting the crafting process was not all that chaotic. For example, the Altamira Axes, excavated in the Altamira Cave in Spain, have a common shape which is shared across all 455 axe heads which comprised the collection, with all of them having identical cuts and chipped-off sections of practically the same shape. The truth is that Paleolithic craftsmen _____.

(a) were not far behind the Neolithic tool-crafting techniques

(b) were in fairly good control of their crafting techniques

(c) created advanced cutting tools just by chipping and cracking

(d) were the most advanced in the Iberian peninsula, like in the Altamira

41. Köln Freistadt was the primary commercial center of northeastern Europe from the 11th century to its fall in 1405. Although the city had only 520 permanent residents, there remains the ruins of three large cathedrals, seven minor chapels, two plazas and numerous commercial and residential structures(houses, stores, stables, etc.), ninety-seven inns and hotels, seven guard barracks and 40km of city walls and a massive government building, all of which is speculated to have accommodated over 300,000 merchants from all over Europe who supported the city's economy. As a result, the city is considered to _____ out of all known cities either in history or in the contemporary times.

(a) have been the most commerce-dependent city

(b) have had the most lucrative commercial goods

(c) a dream for archaeologists seeking fame and fortune

(d) have been by far the most populous city

42. To: US Army Station Camp Henry Logistics Team

Captain Clarice Merleau-ponty

I have realized today that the number of rifles that was relocated to our base was different from what the documents say. My men and I have rechecked the numbers several times, but it seems clear that 7 of the M16A3 rifles we were supposed to receive have gone missing. I am afraid that it may have been taken by hijackers, while the cargo was passing by Jamestown. Sources suggest that _____, which enabled this to happen despite very strict protocols. I request that you alert the military police immediately, before this matter becomes any more serious.

Regards

Lieutenant Commander Michael Foucault

US Army Station Camp Huxley Logistics Team

(a) the hijacker may be very familiar with our security procedures

(b) the hijackers are headed to the military police department

(c) the military police has not yet been informed about the incident

(d) the press may know something about this incident already

43. Modern drug traffickers are constantly inventing many imaginative ways of producing, smuggling and trading drugs, and it seems the current control and surveillance is usually insufficient to counteract them. Since the police department's input of resources into the matter is so small, the police are often too slow to react to new tricks of the trade, which means the drug traffickers are always a step ahead. Consequently, by the time the police find out about a new trick the drug traffickers use, _____.

   (a) they are likely to have already moved onto a new one
   (b) it is only a matter of time before they are tracked down
   (c) they do not have enough men to crack down on them
   (d) they shift their efforts to other available lucrative goods

44. It is very common for people to use poison to eliminate rats and mice in their homes. Just by leaving a few poisoned tablets around the corners of the house, rats, mice and various nuisances are easily gotten rid of without fuss. However, a great many species of rats have already become immune of the chemicals used in typical rat poison. As a result, most mice just fall sick for a week or two then recover, scurrying around behind walls and under the floor once again. Therefore, _____.

   (a) the rats and mice do not find the poison a threat
   (b) it is not recommended to try to get rid of such vermin
   (c) the method is no longer as effective as it used to be
   (d) using poison only strengthens the rats and mice

www.teps19.com

45. Since the 1975 labor riots, the Dian'an Region's local textile industry has been in crisis. Initially, the casualties and collateral damage from such a violent uprising caused the production capacity to decrease sharply. Once the region recovered from the shock, a new problem arose for the local industry: overpowered textile labor unions, which have made the industry much less lucrative and less competitive. Consequently, in order to try to reinvigorate the region's signature texture industry, the regional government Premier Yu Xianmei have suggested _____.

(a) that the labor unions collaborate with the government to further their rights

(b) that the labor laws must be reexamined to prevent unjust labor exploitation

(c) providing government subsidies to textile companies until the issue subsides

(d) that the law must be revised to limit the power of the textile labor union

46. Liquid-State Drive or LSD is a newly invented memory storage system adopted in the most cutting edge computer systems of today. A strange thing about this new technology is that high performance computers with high capacity LSDs tend to malfunction when used in space stations. This is because the liquid state of the drive, which normally allows the drive to change flexibly depending on what sector the necessary data is stored in, makes it float around haphazardly around the computer, causing short circuits and memory corruption.
The weightless state in space stations were not put into consideration when LSD was first invented. Thus, the weightlessness makes the LSDs original advantages _____

_____.

(a) not as effective as it is back down on Earth

(b) possible to be used for different purposes

(c) offset its disadvantages of its liquid state

(d) become a problem that needs to be solved

47. According to the teachings of Bei Tsu, there is one most important factors that decide the harvest of a certain year. It is the frequency and the amount of annual rainfall. He says that the amount of rainfall throughout a year controls the success of the year's harvest. This is shown by the fact that some areas harvest more crops at the end of the year, even though the fertility of the soil was judged to be similar. For example, ancient records show that two fields with similar fertility and different rainfall had significantly different harvests, whereas two fields with similar rainfall and different fertility did not show much difference in the end. The obvious conclusion Bei Tsu made was that rainfall is _____.

(a) the deciding factor in a year's harvest is in the amount of rainfall

(b) irrelevant to deciding how much crops will be harvested that year

(c) detrimental to the growing of rice crops in some very fertile lands

(d) one of the most important factors which decide the fertility of the soil.

48. One December 18, 1992, the thermometers in Svericoldjorn read a record low temperature of -73 degrees Celsius, leaving the power plant and several important electronic equipment out of function, and a large number of people dead due to hypothermia. While the people were stuck in the city, with their cars not starting and heaters not working, the citizens decided to pull down the UNESCO-protected Nordic ruin of Djontsburn, and burn it for fuel. Despite the outrageousness of the idea, this last resort was later accepted and understood worldwide, considering it was the only way to save their lives. From these events, a new provision has been added to the UNESCO cultural heritage regulations, adding that

_____.

(a) a protected cultural heritage site should never be jeopardized

(b) cold regions are henceforth exempt from some of the rules thereof

(c) protection of human life is always a priority to protecting heritage sites

(d) the heritage sites in areas with extreme conditions should be relocated

주제찾기

1. All class-4 personnel contaminated by the microorganism SCP-9983 must consult the facility quarantine officer before leaving the premises. Under the facility quarantine protocol, all associated individuals will undergo a decontamination procedure free of charge, and will be provided with a week's dose of antibacterial tablets. The quarantine department assures you that none of the crew will suffer permanent illness due to the microorganism, and promises insurance for those whose symptoms persist. Please note, however, anyone who violates the protocol will be eliminated.

Q: What is the announcement mainly about?
(a) The actions that will be taken against those who violate the protocol
(b) Reasons why the facility quarantine protocol should be adhered to
(c) The medication that is to be issued to contaminated personnel
(d) A mandatory quarantine protocol for associated staff

2. In his 1433 play The Venetian Flea Chaser, Venetian playwright Lorenzo de Vecco, critically portrayed recent history, something that had never been seen in western literature. He addressed many historical controversies, especially those regarding Italian politics, including the notorious corruption in his home city Venice that once undermined the very foundation of Italian commerce. For Lorenzo, the rising prosperity of the western world during the 15th century could not hide the horrible and wasteful incidents that took place in the previous century.

Q: What is the main topic of the passage?
(a) What socio-historical conflicts Lorenzo predicted
(b) How historical controversies were portrayed in western literature
(c) How greater prosperity of the western world affected renaissance literature
(d) How Lorenzo de Vecco depicted history negatively

3. French gourmet and connoisseur Jean Grandetgras proposed the term "amuse-bouche" in 1963 to name the small, bite-sized dishes which became fashionable recently for master chefs to serve before the meal. He observed that the dish was not ordered from the menu by patrons, but often served freely by the chef's choice alone. The custom soon provided an arena of competition for chefs to show their mastery of cooking. Shortly after, the competition resulted in the chefs using the finest ingredients and the most avant-garde of recipes, that the gourmet named it "amuse-bouche", meaning "mouth amuser".

Q: What is the main idea about Amuse-bouche according to the passage?

(a) The Gourmet Jean Grandetgras first coined the term in 1913

(b) An amuse-bouche is cooked and designed according to the diner's wishes

(c) It was observed by the gourmet that amuse-bouche was often neglected by patrons

(d) Amuse-bouche became very high-quality soon after its introduction, due to competition

4. Interested in working in the most comfortable working environment for you? Work-at-home jobs provide you with a convenient working environment, freedom of attire, and many more advantages. HomeWork will arrange you with companies with working home opportunities according to your career. As soon as you receive our service, you will be discovering yourself free from the intense working atmosphere. Simply leave it to HomeWork and we will bring your work to your home.

Q: What is the advertisement mainly about?

(a) An opportunity to work at home

(b) How to balance out the pros and cons of working at home

(c) A company that introduces work-at-home jobs

(d) A service that provides positions at a prestigious corporations

5. Chlorophyll, a pigment found in the chloroplasts of plant cells, gives plants their green color. It is where photosynthesis takes place, gathering all the sunlight and dioxide, which is crucial for the health of a plant. Similar to chlorophyll are different colored-pigments, such as xanthophylls and carotenoids, which reflect the color of the plant. These pigments are used in photosynthesis as well although they appear in lesser quantities than green chlorophylls. For example, a leaf prevented from receiving sunlight would not be green due to the lack of chlorophyll for photosynthesis.

Q: What is the main topic of the passage?

(a) The process of photosynthesis

(b) Why leaves reflect colors of different pigments

(c) The elements that make plants green

(d) The effects of chlorophyll on plants

6. While the so-called "dumb" phones are disappearing quickly, some other electronic gadgets are disappearing even faster. Digital cameras, portable gaming console, PDAs and mp3 players have almost disappeared off the market since 2010, and they may become completely obsolete by the next few years. The leading factor contributing to their demise is the sheer multi-functionality of smart phones. With their phones becoming more versatile and compact than ever, people are no longer feeling the need for bulky separate devices.

Q: What is the passage mainly about?

(a) The inconvenience of using separate devices

(b) Smartphone's dominance in the electronics market

(c) The disappearance of dumb phones from the market

(d) The versatility and compactness of smartphones

7. With the service at Heckscher, you are completely free from the pain of termites. You simply make a call and relax for a while as our trained professionals eradicate even the miniscule trace of termites with FDA approved chemicals and high quality equipment. Extra services are available for 30 days within the previous session and other options, including the type of chemicals or quick-call service without additional cost, are also available. There are no better options for termite treatments than Heckschers! Call us at 602-4529-0016 right now. Free yourself from the unnecessary pain.

Q: What is mainly being advertised?

(a) A chemical engineering company

(b) A service center that augments the problem of termites

(c) An insect controlling company

(d) A family business run by the Heckschers

8. The terminology, "Quantum physics" is a branch of science dealing with physical phenomena on a diminutive level. It provides a mathematical description of 'particle-like' and 'wave-like' behavior and interactions of energy and matter. In epitome, one of the main ideas of Quantum Theory states that it is physically impossible to know both the position and the particle's momentum at the same time. Another idea of the theory claims that the atomic world is nothing like the world we live in. While these may sound unfamiliar and strange at a glance, Quantum physics provides clues to the field of science and the fundamental nature of the universe.

Q: What is the main topic of the passage?

(a) The ways in which particles and matters interact with one another

(b) Energy decides the momentum of a particle

(c) An overall explanation on Quantum physics

(d) A description on the scientific theories provided by Quantum

9. The phenomenon of group conformity is surprisingly prevalent in various occasions. Despite the fact that an individual knew the answer to a simple test question with certainty, he ended up providing the wrong answer to go along with the crowd. Psychologically, people actually convince themselves that they are thinking what the group is thinking. The tendency is highly probable when in great uncertainty. Also, the feeling of assimilation plays a crucial role in such behavioral inclination. People's primary motivation is to be liked and accepted by others and their greatest fear is to be different and alienated.

Q: What is the passage mainly about?

(a) The feeling of fear that affects one's decision-making process

(b) Experimenting the subject excluded from the majority group

(c) Reasons why an individual had the wrong answer

(d) The attitude and action of the majority having profound influence on individuals

10. During the early 19th century, a style of painting called "Impressionism" emerged from the French art, which had previously been largely academic. It was associated most often with few prominent artists, among whom were Eduard Manet, Claude Monet, and Pierre-Auguste Renoir. The new impressionist art rejected classicism and the French academism. It had a liberal style which would be painted "as it is seen", employing a technique called "en plein air" or "in the open air" hinting the Impressionist tradition of painting casual subjects out in the open. The Impressionist movement significantly influenced the later flow of art, and is noted by some art historians to be the beginning of modern art.

Q: What is the main topic of the passage?

(a) The beginnings of modernism in art

(b) A brief account of the French Impressionist movement

(c) The artists who are most often mentioned in Impressionist art

(b) The influence of French Academism on the French Impressionists

11. A new study suggests that if mothers were to avoid using the microwave, they may have a better chance of preventing cancer in their future children. Researchers, through careful examination of 4000 pregnant women, have concluded that microwaves cause prenatal cancer genes to form in the fetus. They found that every ten minutes of exposure to an operating microwave increases the chance of cancer by one percent. The discovery indicates an evident correlation between microwave exposure and the risk of the future offspring contracting cancer.

Q: What is the passage mainly about?

(a) Microwave exposure can cause infertility in mothers

(b) Microwave ovens increase the risk of cancer in mothers

(c) The need for future children to avoid using the microwave

(d) Exposure to microwaves can increase the chance of cancer in unborn children

12. The SAT scores of the students in my school were all ranked within the top one percent of the nation. Beneath that, however, the desires of the higher group were not much different from those of the lower 99 percent. These overachieving students, whose daily routines never allowed for any significant pastimes, had piles of magazines and game CDs under their beds; Justin Hoover, Starcraft and Playboy were all a part of their hidden treasures. It was as if, despite having no time or apparent desire whatsoever for these mediocre hobbies, they were driven by the same instinct as any other student: to seek something fun.

Q: What is the passage mainly about?

(a) A prestigious school that the writer attended

(b) A reason why we seek fun things even when we are busy

(c) A surprising similarity between the top students and the rest

(d) The hidden treasures of overachieving students within the top one percent

13. Structural stress in aluminum fuselages cause some of the molecular alignment to become condensed. In other words, the originally linear alignment becomes jagged and irregular when structural force is applied. While this change may harmlessly increase the overall durability of the structure, it eventually causes the tensile strength to deteriorate drastically and become dangerously brittle. A research conducted on crashed aircrafts discovered that aluminum fuselages that suffered from prolonged structural stress absorbed less shock from the impact, resulting in higher casualty counts.

Q: What is the main idea of the passage?

(a) Structural stress sometimes strengthens an aluminum structure in the short term

(b) Structural stress is the main cause of many aircraft crashes

(c) Structural stress is detrimental to the structural safety of a fuselage

(d) Prolonged structural stress can have devastating results unless special caution is taken during use

14. Through the last two decades, the number of animals used in scientific experiments and product testing has more than quadrupled. These animals, more than five million of which are used every year, are mostly rodents like mice, guinea pigs, hamsters and squirrels. While human trials and experiments are becoming more and more expensive and politically sensitive, these animals provide a cost-effective and reasonably human-like alternative to humans. However, increased awareness of animal rights have recently made it much more troublesome to perform testing on animals. Furthermore, the increased demand for rodents as pets caused the animals' prices to rise, making it a much less attractive choice.

Q: What is the topic of the passage?

(a) The problems of testing with animals like rodents

(b) The decreased incentive to use animals like rodents as test subjects

(c) A new legislation concerning scientific testing on animals like rodents

(d) The dangers of human testing and its potential political inconveniences

15. The radioactive isotope Tepsium-19 is an uncommon by-product of spontaneous nuclear fission
in stars. It is a useful substance which is essential for the operation of the most common types
of nuclear fission plants across the world, but is unfortunately extremely rare on Earth.
Thus, several powerful nations vied to take a larger share when an abundant reserve of
Tepsium-19 was reported to have been discovered on the surface of the Moon in 1969.
In addition, global energy conglomerates started lobbying their governments, each competing
for an exclusive contract and mining rights. All this fuss subsided, however, when subsequent
trips to the moon proved that the alleged Tepsium-19 reserve was found out to be Toefleum-19,
which had a similar emission spectrum indistinguishable by existing technologies.

Q: What is the main topic of the passage?

(a) The usefulness of the radioactive isotope Tepsium-19

(b) A disputed rare resource reserve on the surface of the Moon

(c) A worldwide competition for a rare resource that never existed

(d) A historical power struggle between nations and corporate powers

16. Recent studies indicate that wiggling one's toes may be much more effective an exercise than
previously thought. They claim that just wiggling one's toes for 30 minutes a day can make
you lose weight and help prevent diabetes, arthritis and even penile atrophy. A thorough test on
300 individuals of diverse physical conditions proved that an average of 100kcal was lost when
they wiggled their toes for 60 minutes, and that it removed about 603mg of harmful chemicals
like Tepsium from the body. These astounding numbers exceed even that of weightlifting and
jogging. This is an exciting new discovery for those fitness-seekers as no other exercises that can
be done on-the-go have been proven to have more efficacy than toe wiggling.

Q: What is the best title for this passage?

(a) The Horrifying Effects of Diabetes, Arthritis and Penile Atrophy

(b) Toe-wiggling Exercise Extremely Helpful for Preventing Various Diseases

(c) A Complete Guide to Burning Fat and Getting Rid of Harmful Chemicals

(d) A New Form of Exercise Found to Have Considerable Effectiveness for Fitness

17. Dear Student

We would first like to congratulate you for being selected as this year's student of the year. Your academic achievements and philanthropic spirit is no doubt exemplar for all of our students. Therefore, we are delighted to invite you to the 2013 Jamestown-Surley Dinner Party, where you will meet, dine and talk with renowned academics from diverse fields. Furthermore, you will be asked to give the starting speech for the event, which is an honor rarely given to students. Please do not miss this precious life opportunity; we assure you that it will become one of the most unforgettable moments in your entire life.

Frederick Paritzche Professor

California Institute of Technology

Q: What is the main idea of the letter?

(a) The student has been nominated for the student of the year award

(b) The college will be holding a meeting between famous academics this year

(c) The student in question has been invited to a very special event

(d) The 2013 Jamestown College Dinner Party will be very memorable

18. To all Jamestown residents

Sightings of a mentally ill man holding a rifle has been reported several times over the last few days. It is not yet clear who the man may be and how he gained access to his rifle, but it is suspected that he is the man who escaped from the mental asylum last week. The police say they are currently searching for this crazy man, and the situation is under control. Fortunately, there have not been any shootings or accidents, but the police warns that his rifle is apparently loaded and cocked, and the mental asylum records show that he is a retired veteran army officer with a condition of paranoia. Please stay indoors and keep your doors locked until the madman is captured and arrested by the local police.

Clyfford de Stijl

Town Mayor

Q: What is the purpose of the announcement?

(a) To collect more evidence for tracking down an insane man

(b) To warn people not to leave their houses because of a danger

(c) To ask people to cooperate with the police's search mission

(d) To investigate where the insane man obtained his rifle

19. After several tragic accidents, the public antipathy toward guns has much grown. One of the primary causes of this change was due to a catastrophic gun rampage in a college event last year, which killed 45 and injured hundreds. The increase in the number of minor gun accidents in general has been one of the reasons of the escalating stigma towards guns. Such movements has also been stimulated by the Self-Defense Act that passed congress last month, which loosened qualification standards required to carry concealed-carry weapons and made it no longer illegal to hold guns in some public premises like colleges. Also the increased popularity of peace oriented cults also has stimulated this rising tension.

Q: What is the passage mainly about?

(a) Tragic incidents involving shootings which took place last year

(b) The relationships between public consensus and media coverage

(c) Weapon related regulations and its effect on the public's sentiments

(d) Factors that caused people to have a negative opinion for guns

20. In 1985, the National Land Swimming Championships Committee was established as the nation's first land swimming competition host. The first land swimming race, which was held on the Paddington Olympics Stadium, took place soon after the Committee was founded. Five years after this event in 1990, an even bigger land swimming competition was held in Los Angeles, and the sport enjoyed the pinnacle of its popularity, far exceeding that of baseball and football. The popular sport took a sharp downturn, however, when it was found in 1992 that the committee was manipulating the game results for monetary gains. As time progressed, the people slowly forgot about the sport, and now very few people remember that such a sport even existed.

Q: What is the passage mainly about?

(a) The dangers of swimming on land without proper equipment

(b) The beginning of a new popular sport which prospered in the 90s

(c) The decline of a popular sport due to accusations of game rigging

(d) The astounding speed in which people can forget about past issues

21. The National "Cats as Pets" movement has risen along with the general tendency to popularize pet animals that arose and became mainstream from 2010 up until now. The videos produced by the partakers of this movement intended to awaken people to the irresistible cuteness of cats and encourage the keeping of cats as pets. The leaders of this movement used various methods such as Facebook and Twitter to create imaginary anthropomorphic cat personalities which would continually post pictures of its "friends". Although the beginning of this movement is unclear, it is usually thought that it was the popularization of SNS media which allowed it to become easily known to the greater public.

Q: What is the main topic of the passage?

(a) The popularity of cats as pets from around 2010

(b) The beginning of the National Cats as Pets Movement

(c) The importance of cats in the general tendency of the time

(d) The prosperity of cats as imaginary pets through the SNS media

쏘아보기
적용
실전문제

빈 칸 채 우 기

1. The Japanese economy _____ during the 1960s and 70s. Skyscrapers could be seen in the midst of Tokyo for the first time. Men started to wear suits to become more respected in their businesses and because they could afford them. The general standard of living increased greatly in every aspect as well.

(a) developed at an eye-popping rate

(b) went through a recession

(c) became more globalized

(d) succeeded in overcoming a depression

2. Choi's Preowned Automobiles boasts a new hybrid line of used cars, comprising of many famous brands like Hyundai, Kia, and Toyota. Newly incorporated in the line is the famous 2012 Toyota Prius. The one year old fuel-efficient car has the following features such as a 40 km per liter fuel efficiency, a sleek and sophisticated design, and an affordable price. Moreover, drivers are better protected with the superior warranty of Toyota that non-Toyota drivers envy. So come down to Choi's _____.

(a) for the all new 2012 Toyota Prius

(b) to purchase our new Hyundai models

(c) if you wish to gain information about a partnership with Choi's

(d) for more information about hybrid cars

3. In South Korea, _____. South Koreans, mostly the younger
generations, have the conception that an individual's blood type influences his or her personality.
For instance, if your blood type is A, you are then more likely to be introverted. However,
this false perception can sometimes have a negative impact in building relationships because a
person's blood type can lead to a prejudice when establishing a first impression.

(a) many people have some sort of a blood phobia

(b) there is a unique biased culture regarding blood types

(c) the older generation tends to emphasize blood types

(d) scientists have tricked the citizens into believing the myth about blood types

4. Nevertheless, it is nowadays common to see teenage or college girls disregard such side effects
and visit plastic surgeons. As lookism and discrimination according to someone's facial and
bodily features are becoming rampant, procedures of plastic surgery have become the solution to
this appearance-oriented society no matter what the repercussions are. Such phenomena sharply
shows _____.

(a) the outcome of overdoing plastic surgery

(b) the close connection of extreme "lookism" and success in society

(c) the unpleasant situation of plastic surgery in a beauty-infatuated society

(d) how plastic surgery can make you famous

5. The wildlife conservatory located in Bronx Zoo is currently operating a program for children to
_____. However, many young students residing in New York
City are still unaware of the current state of various endangered animals in the United States.
Thus, in order to increase awareness for these children, the conservatory is conducting weekly
classes that enable students to learn about different animals facing extinction. The activities
require children to tour around the zoo to find endangered species, learn about their living
habits, and find ways to improve their conditions.

(a) help take care of animals in the zoo
(b) give attention to animals who are close to facing extinction
(c) understand what aspects of New York City are negative for animal habitation
(d) figure out the reasons behind the animal behavior all around the states

6. Trying to _____? Take a vacation at the Tamazaai Islands!
You can swim all day, read books near the fireplace and get a tan near the beach. Just pay $150,
and you will get 2 free tickets. Enjoy the life of luxury that you would not be able to have in
your everyday life. For additional service, we give you a free meal at the Rest-in Palace Hotel,
which is the best hotel in the Tamazaai Islands. Get your tickets right now!

(a) enjoy a luxurious vacation at a cheap price
(b) get 2 free tickets to the Tamazaai Islands
(c) find a place to visit on summer break
(d) find the best area for sight seeing

7. The Korean _____. Samsung Electronics is playing a big role in this area, with its innovative ideas shaping the lifestyles of the ordinary people. Its recent release of the Galaxy 4 Series has been receiving positive appeal not only in the local market, but also in the international market. People now get to enjoy new technologies which make their daily lives more efficient and convenient.

(a) economy is led by a few major IT companies

(b) IT companies are affecting the lives of the global population

(c) government is striving for new ways to develop technology

(d) market is declining due to the recent economic crisis

8. Forensic psychologists around the world are distressed because of _____ _____. A year ago, a series of murders, which are thought to have been carried out by one person, was committed in the capital city of Spain, Madrid. The pattern of these particular crimes had never been seen before. The development of criminal profiling had allowed psychologists to analyze criminals' minds in deeper and more profound manner than ever. Applied to this case however, it showed its limits. The profiling was useless in ascertaining the primary motive of the Madrid serial killer as such behavior had never been seen in serial murder cases.

(a) the limitation of the law enforcement authority in Madrid

(b) the ineffectiveness of conventional forensic psychology

(c) the pressure of the urgency to catch a criminal

(d) series of baffling cases of criminal actions

9. HawkVision, the most advanced technology on the market, is here to increase the impartiality in a tennis match. Using 8 ultra-high speed cameras which are installed around the tennis court, the cameras are always prepared to keep the game fair for the players and fans and to relieve the umpires of pressures of making difficult decisions. Combining the visions from all 8 cameras, the movement of the tennis ball is recorded and a 3D video image is downloaded in a database which can be shown immediately on the electronic scoreboard. The HawkVision allows

_____.

(a) the umpire to prevent a player from cheating

(b) the umpire to keep the players from injuries.

(c) the game to be carried out fair and square.

(d) people to see tennis games in max 8 courts.

10. A lot of inventions and technology that people use on a daily basis _____

_____. For example, the post-it note paper was not something that the developers first had in mind. Originally, they were trying to create a powerful heavy-duty glue, but a newly hired assistant mistakenly mixed in the wrong chemicals which produced glue that would barely stick paper together. Ironically, however, that failed invention became insanely popular when it was applied to a note paper which made it possible to easily attach and detach from all surfaces without residue.

(a) weren't expected to be profitable

(b) are from developers of the post-it notes

(c) were expected to rake in money

(d) are from serendipitous discoveries.

11. A new advancement in technology has major paper companies struggling to make ends meet. We live in the digital era, where everything from books to formal contracts are produced and stored electronically. Whereas people had to carry heavy paperback books or documents in paper form in the past, everything now fits perfectly inside electronic handheld devices in the form of digital files. As more and more people are starting to buy E-books or electronic books, experts claim with some certainty that paper books _____.

(a) are becoming more popular than ever before

(b) are no different from e-books

(c) may become obsolete very soon

(d) are products of human ingenuity

12. During this year's budget review meeting, the student council president noticed a critical flaw that exposed _____. While going through last year's financial records related to allocation of club funds, she recognized that sports clubs received over 70 percent of the total budget, despite the fact that they only account for about 15 percent of total clubs. This forced cultural and religious clubs to operate solely based on the private funds collected from the members.

(a) an unfair distribution of club funds

(b) a need to augment the overall budget for club activities

(c) an abrupt change in the school's budgetary policy

(d) incidents where certain clubs were unilateral shutdowns

13. Culinary touristy is an innovative technique of travel in which tourists focus solely on the traditional food and cuisine of another region. Essentially, travelers mainly target the eatery rather than any other aspect of a foreign country. For example, a person visiting a South African province will visit local towns where they can experience ethnic food tastings or partake in cooking classes conducted by an original inhabitant. This traveling technique is not just a technique used by people who have professional training in the culinary field. It is _____.

(a) used as a way of experts gaining more knowledge in this area

(b) regarded as a traveling method that anyone interested in this field can enjoy

(c) best known for decreasing the difficulties that travelers experience

(d) used in enhancing the cooking abilities of chefs

14. Dear Senator Kim,

I have read your proposal you submitted to Congress last fall. With all due respect, however I disagree with your decision to allocate a number of parking spaces designated for solely female drivers. As a fellow driver, I believe that it is absolutely unfair and irrational. What I am most discordant about is that the number of female parking spots considerably exceeds the number of handicap parking spots. Policies like this will encourage radical feminism in the country. I sincerely ask you to _____.

Sincerely,

Gil Dong, Hong

(a) reconsider your policy before this country becomes sexually biased

(b) enforce your policy to help female drivers

(c) make new parking spots designated for males

(d) suspend your policy until we hear the opinions of female drivers

15. The debut of the avant-garde filmmaker Stevie Collins and his film, Runaway Boys, resulted in the audience discovering a new realm in the topic of AIDS. Collins's ultimate goal of this controversial film was for people to alter their perceptions of AIDS patients. Instead of identifying this group of people as filthy and shallow-minded in their sexual relationships, they should be seen as no different from any other kinds of long-term disease patients. With no astonishment, his film has swiftly led to the argument in

_____.

(a) the justification of prejudice against people suffering with AIDS

(b) whether this film appropriately deals with sexual relations

(c) which approach is better in treating AIDs patients

(d) the need for a complete change in the films dealing with AIDS

16. Our privacy on the internet is increasingly being invaded as technology is progressing. The emergence of various Social Networking Services has made it practicable for exposure of personal information to the public. Accessing a specific person's address or phone number in an incomparably short period of time is now possible for anyone using services like Facebook. This invasion to other people's privacy has become taken for granted by so many people that many people no longer find it rude or disrespectful to pry into other people's personal information. Unlike the past, _____.

(a) Social networking services are available for all kinds of people

(b) People are vulnerable to fraud from social networking services

(c) Privacy penetration has been perceived to be something natural

(d) There are more people joining into internet communities

17. One of the first color movies was shown on the big screen in France in 1934. The title of the movie was House and one of the most famous actors of all time, Jack Sparrow, starred in it. Due to lack of technology and financial support, House did not display spectacular lights and actions that movies nowadays do. However, colors on the big screen were a sensational shock to movie goers then, to whom black and white movies were the norm. As a result, the movie topped the film charts for more than a year. House definitely is _____

_____.

(a) one of the worst movies in cinema history.

(b) comparable in its qualities to the blockbusters of these days.

(c) a masterpiece for the great actor Jack Sparrow.

(d) a milestone in the business of TV series.

18. It is a common misunderstanding that establishing many relationships with people can help one in overcoming an illness. In fact, it has been found in a research that what is more important is _____. The research was conducted by Amie Song, a distinguished professor at Harvard Medical School in Massachusetts. According to Song, although having numerous relationships might seem to help the patient at first, shallow relationships and meetings eventually leave the patient with a sense of futility, thereby worsening the illness. Having a deep and intimate relationship with even just one person can greatly increase the chance of overcoming an ailment.

(a) the level of medical support one is receiving.

(b) the will to overcome the sickness.

(c) having friends to cover for one's medical expenses.

(d) the depth and intimacy of the relationships.

19. As a leading company in space travels, Easy Space now provides civilians with opportunities to travel into space. With our ion-propelled rocket engine and launch platforms in 30 countries around the world, you may start your travel to the moon in less than a day. All the technology and equipment have been certified by NASA and the highest level of safety is guaranteed. Contact our travel agent now _____.

(a) to find out how many civilians traveled to the moon

(b) why ion-propelled rocket engines are better than fossil fueled ones

(c) for advice to creating your own rocket engines

(d) for a quick and safe trip to space

20. Cadets chosen as members of the Bluerock Project are _____. Moving in secrecy to effectuate higher orders is the ultimate target of the Bluerock Project, and all constituents are asked to please render themselves to fulfill this motion. The individual policies and agendas on proper comportment will be stated in the confidential files accessible to only the cadets involved. We command all cadets to heed by the orders. Without exceptions, violations of the policies will result in expulsion.

(a) provided with financial aid nationally

(b) obliged to abide by the edict

(c) free to trespass the headquarters with an authorized identification

(d) required to follow highly confidential governmental orders

21. Mehlenbacher's *Human* is a book that _____. The objective of this publication is criticism on the stereotypical assumption that humans are all self-centered. With reference to Hsun-tzu and Hobbes, Mehlenbacher refutes the points claimed both in the oriental and western society. Mehlenbacher also descriptively explains the social background that led to concluding human's nature in a misconstrued way.

(a) is acknowledged for its political views on moral characteristics
(b) sarcastically ridicules human's fundamentally good nature
(c) uses metaphors to portray about egocentrism
(d) contradicts the misconception of human's innate personality

22. Last year, the Supreme Court finally ruled "bullying" as a criminal offense, prompting more draconian rules against bullying in high schools. Not only physical violence but also verbal abuse and cyber bullying can be prosecuted under the new law. This means that school administrators and teachers must now report to police authorities when confronted with a case of bullying. This has, however, resulted in a phenomenon where schools ignore cases of bullying, fearing that they may damage the school's reputation. For such reasons, the Ministry of Education is considering _____.

(a) a policy allowing schools to handle bullying cases by themselves
(b) a surprise police visit to all high schools across the country
(c) to lower the rate of cyber bullying in schools by conducting a scan of school computers
(d) the expulsion of students who are bullied

23. There are many ways to _____. Any small helping hand is actually a huge contribution. You can erase the blackboard before the start of each session. You can also make sure that all the technological equipment is in order. Even simple acts such as these will be a great help to your classmates and your teacher and will thus be highly appreciated.

(a) give help to your teacher

(b) get involved in your classroom setting

(c) get along with your classmates

(d) earn the respect of your teacher.

24. Up until the First World War, also known as the Great War, people still considered war to be a glorious thing. Many texts and books from that time, 1914, suggest that people were actually excited with the beginning of a war. People saw this as a chance to show that they were washed away from their selfishness and wanted to show patriotism and dedication for their country. However the brutality of this war changed this conception and so _____ _____.

(a) war became something to be feared rather than looked forward to

(b) war was the symbol of energy and glory

(c) World War 2 broke out soon after

(d) more and more people enlisted in the forces

25. My Dearest Sarah

I have thought long and hard and I have made up my mind. Our years together have been marvelous together and I want nothing more than it to go on. I will not lie in saying that family pressure has also been a factor in my decision since I once believed a man should not be tied down to one woman. But I feel like you are the right one for me. Therefore, I want

_____.

(a) for you and I to break up

(b) to stop lying to my parents

(c) to be your husband

(d) to go back to college

26. In 1996 just 6% of the planet's inhabitants spoke English as a first language, while 96% of all e-commerce websites were written primarily in English. However, companies soon realized that, in order to target foreign markets, they needed to create sites with local languages and content. It was the only way they could truly maximize global revenues. This meant that local web designers fluent in English were _____.

(a) encouraged to study web design

(b) increasingly in high demand

(c) restricted to a few specialties

(d) subject to greater competition

27. Patients of chronic fatigue syndrome (CFS) experience severe and prolonged tiredness or weariness. According to some researchers it could be caused by a virus, perhaps what is called herpes virus-6. Others think the immune response or the autoimmune process is to blame for causing CFS by inflammations of nervous system pathways. All we can safely say is that

_____.

(a) the cases of CFS have not increased since

(b) CFS continues to be regarded as a rare syndrome.

(c) the exact causes of CFS remain unknown

(d) CFS research still suffers from poor funding

28. At Vets Plus, we have embarked on a strategy to diversify our products and enhance our mission of providing the best possible medical care for animals. To this end, we have partnered with several companies and our valued partners now include the National Animal Hospital Association, Network of Professional Veterinarians, and Animal Friends Market Researchers. Vets Plus is proud of the fact that such fine organizations have joined us in sharing a passion for providing high-quality animal care. If you are interested in _____, please contact our Marketing Department at 814-466-0542.

(a) the best veterinary service to customers

(b) a partnership with our organization

(c) new products that customers will appreciate

(d) introducing us to veterinarians who meet our standards

29. A long-standing distinction exists between "fine art" and "folk art" in the world of art. The distinction is based on the idea that fine art is the kind of art made for aesthetic appreciation, produced by trained artists for its beauty rather than for something more practical. This implies that all other art is more appropriately called "folk" or "ethnic" art. Such art _____. Traditionally it had been practiced by unschooled artists for the purpose of adorning domestic items, such as pottery, as well as artifacts used for cultural rituals and in warfare.

(a) tends to be created for its own specific purpose

(b) fulfills a decorative or an utilitarian purpose

(c) relies on the rejection of formal traditions

(d) competes with pieces of fine art in the market

30. People's moods affect _____. For example, when people are angry, their attention is narrowly focused on the person or thing that is upsetting them and they have only a little room for input from another source. Thus, it is a good idea to not approach a co-worker regarding an important issue when he or she is irritated or feeling down because you will not get the attention you deserve. In the same sense, when feeling cheerful, people are typically much more receptive to input.

(a) the sharpness of the criticism they offer

(b) their feelings toward those around them

(c) the manner in which they convey ideas

(d) their ability to absorb information

31. Most armadillos _____. When they are first born, their skin is soft and fragile which makes it challenging for them to protect themselves from predators. This makes their survival strenuous when they are young. However, as their bodies grow longer and wider about two or three weeks after birth, the armadillos form plates composed of bone and layered with horns. When a month passes and the plates are fully grown, they play a crucial role in the defense mechanism of many armadillos, and as they escape from predators into patches of thorns, they are protected by their armored plates.

(a) utilize escaping methods when faced with predators

(b) are able to attack the predators with their horns

(c) have no ability to catch prey

(d) lack ways of defense until they mature physically

32. During my stay in Lithuania, people's sensitivity in giving flowers as gifts was bewildering for me. The most idealistic way of giving flowers is sending an odd number of flowers in a wrapping of bright colors such as red and yellow, yet people seldom followed that traditional custom. Nevertheless, there was an incident in which I brought chrysanthemums for a party host and received unpleasant looks from him, which made me baffled. On another occasion, I had brought a bundle of white flowers for my friend's birthday, and only realized afterwards that white flowers are strictly reserved for weddings. Giving flowers as gifts _____ _____.

(a) was very helpful when trying to acquaint with new people

(b) is deemed useful only for wedding occasions.

(c) requires a knowledge of several etiquettes regarding the act

(d) should not be encouraged for health purposes

33. Most people are aware of the fact that 'one-ingredient diet', a dietary plan based on only consuming one ingredient, is often times fatal to health. Luckily, experts in this field have derived a more effective yet healthier diet method that has been named the "penta-ingredient diet". Success stories on this new diet technique are currently sprouting from many different regions in the United States. The main idea of the 'penta-ingredient diet' is that five different food products should be chosen and consumed equally on a daily basis. When following this diet, people should _____. For example, if a person chooses apples as one of their five ingredients, bananas should be disregarded as being another food product.

(a) focus on choosing the most filling ingredient

(b) understand how tiresome it is to start a strict diet

(c) give priority to fruits over others when choosing the five food products

(d) find each food product from different food criteria

34. Dear Sebastian,

Why do couples always have to celebrate petty events like New Years Day or Valentines Day? I have a girlfriend that I have been in a relationship with for 2 years already, and I feel that such events do not truly reflect the love I have for the other person. In fact, those events are artificial, and do not demonstrate true affection. Never have I in the past celebrated such events with my girlfriend. It still upsets me when _____.

Is there a problem in thinking this way?

Sincerely,

Jack

(a) my girlfriend agrees with me

(b) my friends criticize me for not celebrating those events

(c) my friends say that Valentine's Day is artificial

(d) I receive presents from my girlfriend

35. _____ has resulted from a chronological observation of different countries around the world. Social scientists have concluded that industrialization first began in Great Britain. During the next decade, usage of machines, which ignited the process of industrialization, spread to other European countries such as France, Italy, and Poland. Gradually, Asian and North American countries began to be industrialized as well, as they became colonized by European countries that had prospered and grown through industrialization. Today, most countries around the world are industrialized.

(a) The understanding of the development of industrialization

(b) Proof of increase in globalization

(c) The information cycle of industrialization

(d) Evidence that industrialization didn't occur in Asia

36. The article above summarizes the progress made in the United States to resolve the national problem of obesity. Some states have attempted to reduce obesity by introducing state-wide policies to implement low-calorie lunch programs in schools, which has successfully lowered obesity rates. However, smaller and low-budgeted states have found it too costly to introduce state-wide low-calorie lunch programs. Therefore, _____.

(a) more research is no longer necessary for a solution

(b) high school and middle school students must cooperate

(c) funding is required in order to reduce obesity nationwide

(d) progress in decreasing obesity rates has been outstanding

37. Last year my Labrador was involved in a car crash that left his forelegs broken. Despite taking him to the veterinarian immediately, the damage was proven to be much too severe for treatment, leading to an amputation of both legs. We tried to make life as comfortable as possible for him, but it was simply too devastating to see him unable to walk. Therefore after several weeks, we decided to euthanize him. Fortunately, we were told upon arrival that a new medical procedure could give him prosthetic legs. Although very costly and exhausting, the procedure was successful and now _____.

(a) our Labrador has been put to sleep

(b) our Labrador still has trouble walking

(c) our Labrador is enjoying his new legs, running around happily

(d) we have been compensated for the crash

38. Hats were a fundamental feature of male fashion for several decades in the Victorian Age, during which men had to wear chadors that covered the entire body except for the eyes. Hats acted as more than just a necessary item, however. Although men during this time were prohibited from expressing themselves because it would violate social principles, they could express emotions by wearing different colors of hats. In other words, men _____

_____.

(a) wore only one type of hat

(b) who had no hats had only one way of expressing themselves

(c) from the Victorian Age wore colored hats

(d) utilized hats as a way of unique communication

39. Researchers have found that _____. They state that the explosion of nuclear plants in Fukushima has caused a leakage of an enormous amount of radioactive substances into the Pacific Ocean, and that these substances have gradually spread to other oceans, leading to a massive accumulation of radioactive substances in marine organisms. As humans are at the top of the food chain, these substances will eventually accumulate in our bodies, causing various health problems.

(a) the health of millions of Japanese is at risk

(b) the seafood market will experience a recession

(c) many nuclear plants need to be shut down

(d) radioactive substances cause health problems

40. Biochemist Erica Watson from the Centre for Trophoblast Research at the University of Cambridge revealed that Folic acid deficiency can stimulate serious health issues in an offspring, including spina bifida and placental abnormalities. Although the pernicious effect of folic acid deficiency was well known, the causation for these detrimental effects on the health of an offspring was not determined. However, through this research, researchers have discovered how the molecular mechanism of folic acid deficiency impacted development, thereby causing health problems. They concluded that when either the maternal grandmother or grandfather had the 'Mtrr mutation', their genetically standard grandchildren had a high possibility of inheriting a diverse range of developmental abnormalities. Thus, the research led by Dr. Watson _____.

(a) gives us a concrete explanation on the health effects of Folic acid deficiency

(b) fails in investigating the reason of abnormalities

(c) hides nothing in revealing the problem of Mtrr mutation

(d) shows the original qualities of the Folic acid deficiency

41. Freidberger & Parks has always been number one in providing the optimum financing and investing solutions in consulting programs of internationally prominent corporations and organizations. We behold an incomparable databank and the utmost consultants to give you the best services and finance solutions for strong- holding your company. Whatever you desire, from professional help forming adroit strategies to financial management of your company, you can count on Freidberger & Parks. Contact us now _____.

(a) to make an appointment with our manager

(b) to register for an orientation regarding recruitments at Freidberger & Parks

(c) for unerring tactics on vested interests in operating your corporation

(d) for more information on the international companies and organizations we work with

42. In the 1930s it was difficult for Korean students to learn their own native language. South Korea was colonized by Japan and many students were forced to conceal their Korean identities and embrace Japanese names. Learning their native language was out of the question. Students using Korean would be harshly punished and sometimes expelled. It is no wonder, therefore, that Koreans became very sensitive to learning Japanese these days. They understood _____.

(a) the sad history of language use in Korea

(b) the importance of learning foreign languages

(c) the history of military conflicts

(d) the importance of being bilingual

43. The National Basketball Association is finally getting serious about _____.
Roy Hibbert of the Indiana Pacers was fined $20,000 the other day for the use of swear words and insults against sports reporters during a press conference. Kobe Bryant was also fined a substantial amount of money by the league last month after belligerently undermining a reporter. The biggest fine in league history, however, was issued when Ron Artest of the Los Angeles Lakers punched a sports reporter for 'crossing the line'. The NBA hopes that the series of fines will somewhat help restore peace to the league.

(a) protecting the reputation and safety of sports reporters
(b) regulating what players say in public
(c) educating its players to have better manners
(d) collecting money from its players

44. Dear Gloria,

Amsterdam has been great so far. There are so many places to see and so many places to take photos that I feel like I never have enough battery left on my phone. By the way, there was one queer experience during my stay at the Hotel of Opera. The name sounded interesting since I have always been a huge fan of opera. However, the reason for its name was because apparently there is a huge opera house adjacent to the hotel, hence the "Hotel of Opera". As a result, I was barely able to sleep from all the loud noises from the venue. Next time, I will make sure to _____.

(a) learn more about Amsterdam
(b) take more photos when I visit a new city
(c) go to a hostel instead of a hotel
(d) research in advance and never assume

45. It was found in a research that children mingle and interact differently when

_____. Children perceive and treat their peers in rather

different ways. Conversing and solving problems together is preferred and they also study

on their own less frequently in comparison to adults. In addition, because children are less

competitive than adults, they see each other as companions rather than competitors.

(a) at night than they do during the day

(b) being taught by an adult

(c) having conversations while studying

(d) studying in groups than adults do

46. I, James White, on behalf of the townspeople, _____.

A recent research conducted by a team of urban engineers revealed that the new construction

by I&C Company will greatly affect the local ecosystem. The parking space planned to be

built would be placed over an area of Atwood Woods, meaning that the construction will

require lumbering of the precious Sequoia trees. These trees are indispensable as they play the

most important role in keeping the nearby ecosystem healthy. Anyone who wants to support

the petition is asked to please sign it at the city hall before July 25th.

(a) ask for a transfer of the Sequoia Trees

(b) demand that the new trees be planted in town

(c) am joining the I&C Company to help with the construction

(d) appeal an official petition over the new parking lot

47. Andrews, our international law firm _____. That is because we recognize that our client may have been wrongly discriminated and the future of an individual might depend on our performance in court. Furthermore, our law firm has a very low acceptance rate of clients, only accepting those who are truly innocent yet suffering. When it comes to defending our client and deliberating on what rights have been exploited, our law firm is impeccable. Without doubt, we will continue to endeavor to remain as a global guardian of those in need. Andrews-the law firm for the world.

(a) has been growing upon remarkable winning records

(b) protects rights at a lower expense than competing firms

(c) offers a comfortable environment for clients

(d) is unquestionably the ideal agency for victimized citizens globally

48. Funafuti spear illustration developed among Tuvaluans during the Paleolithic age. Since then, people have engraved the ancient legends of the Tuvaluans on their sacred spears. Therefore, the study of spear art can unfold the anthropological aspects of the Funafuti culture and history. Indeed, a number of recently unearthed spears were useful in drawing clues to the anthropocentric backgrounds. For example, they contain intricate depictions of its major gods that held considerable significance. Because of their distinctive traits, Funafuti spears _____.

(a) show the number of different tribes present then

(b) stand for people's natural yearning to leave records of their history

(c) represent the importance of spears as weapons

(d) offer some insight into the Tuvaluans' lifestyle

49. The majority of what botanists know about Poreugineyi and its idiosyncrasy to nourish on insects was detected by a science team from Spain partnered by the Institute of New Guinea. Studies found that the environment this plant dwells in affected the diet of this flower, causing it to feed on insects that reproduced in this region. The increase in species of the Poreugineyi was triggered by the excessive consumption of proteins, which exceeded the number of gnats present. Indeed, the science team concluded in a recent examination that the insect populations were at a great downfall due to the plant's habitat. As a result, scientists presume that _____.

(a) species can evolve externally to survive in an environment

(b) more types of flowers are going to be present than originally thought

(c) the environment can change the flower's eating habits

(d) it is likely that insects will go extinct in the near future

50. The Vesuvian Martial Arts routine has been widely assumed to suppress the appetite of an individual performing the art form. After ongoing experiments on the hunger rates of the individuals, researchers at the Ministry of Health in Battanuihi have finally confirmed the norm to be valid. However, what they have not been able to identify is whether the cause for this phenomenon is the uptempo style of movement or the repetitive bobbing motion of the head in the routine. But there also remains a possibility that both factors _____ _____.

(a) will lead the Ministry of Health to find a feasible solution

(b) cause the uptempo movements

(c) are being overlooked in the research

(d) are equally responsible for the decrease in the craving for food

51. Beware tourists! Summer vacation is coming soon, so when you tour around the country, you should be careful of local bugs called Bezlies. Bezlies bites are poisonous and are most rampant during this time of year, which means that you should always be cautious. Otherwise, immense problems such as swelling of skin may arouse. Once you get bitten, it can be time consuming and expensive to treat the damaged skin. For these reasons, it is highly crucial that you _____.

(a) look around 24/7 to see if bugs are flying near you

(b) abstain from scratching the bitten area of your skin

(c) protect your skin by being cautious of bug bites

(d) clean your entire household interior before you go on a trip

52. Before the unification of Germany which occurred on 1871, West and East Germany _____. The Germans had very skilled beer brewers, who had developed different types of beer ranging from pale beers to dark beers with the use of special brewing technology. As a consequence, the quality of beer was superior to that of other European nations. Furthermore, the education system was well established, with a literacy rate of more than 90 percent. The government institutions also made sure that the living standards of every individual met the minimal standards. Therefore, it can be said that even before unification, the East and West Germans lived under a stable government.

(a) were under serious conflict

(b) had an incredibly diverse population

(c) faced tremendous governmental problems

(d) had a stable government with suitable cultural and social infrastructure

53. With the continuous rise in crime rate, government officials are taking significant measures to regulate neighborhood districts and the CCTV's in every major city. Unfortunately, such intervention by the government has not received unanimous support from the community. In fact, official John Walters overturned the proposal to increase the amount of CCTVs with better technology due to its financial burden. If this situation is to continue, it will make it difficult for the police to _____.

(a) move into major cities

(b) track down criminal offenses occurring in the government

(c) monitor the population

(d) propose financial inustments on technology

54. Cicadas make loud and noisy sounds by singing, and scientists have come to believe that these sounds act as mating calls. However, scientists were curious about the way in which each species of cicadas were able to communicate only amongst the same species. To answer this question, scientists placed sound sensors in and around the cicadas' homes to observe their singing moments. Not only were the loud noises made in times of danger, but they were also used to gather together. Scientists hope such an experiment would clarify how

_____.

(a) gathering only occurs when male cicadas sing

(b) cicadas are vulnerable to attacks when singing

(c) female cicadas prefer male cicadas of their own kind

(d) different species of cicadas are not able to communicate with each other

55. Although Alexander the Great's once powerful empire during the Hellenistic period was torn into pieces at the time of its decline, King Alexander is still known for _____ _____. Besides from his military conquests, he sought ways to increase trade between the East and the West to spread the influence of the Greek civilization throughout his empire. As a result, he managed to establish city-states modeled on Greek institutions that came to be major cultural centers long after his death.

(a) his coercive military actions to his neighbouring states

(b) overcoming neighbours' hostility toward Greek culture

(c) economic prosperity through trades between East and West

(d) leaving traces of the expansion of Greek influences

56. After his investigation on the economic gap around the globe, Leonie Schultheiss, a German professor, published a research paper emphasizing _____. The common norm that laziness is the determinant of poverty in developing countries was proven to be an inaccurate analysis. Schultheiss asserted that they are actually more entrepreneurial and found it ironical that those of poor countries were more creative and possessed greater potential to succeed and become rich.

(a) ignorance on the importance of entrepreneurship by rich countries

(b) the necessity of empathizing with poor countries

(c) a paradox in the character of developing countries

(d) developing countries living in poverty because of their entrepreneurship

57. Martin Luther wrote the Ninety-Five Thesis when Germany was _____.
He challenged the authority of the Pope and criticized the sale of indulgences by the Roman Catholic Church. He strongly opposed the believers' purchase of indulgences, which were used to absolve the buyers from all punishments and grant them salvation. Also, Luther argued that people were doubtful about their faith and desired false assurances. To sell indulgences, the church emphasized that the benefits of good works could be obtained by donating money to the church.

(a) facing severe economic downturn due to the sale of indulgences.

(b) increasingly becoming doubtful about the Roman Catholic Church

(c) confident about their relationship with both God and the pope.

(d) uncertain about belief in God and began relying on indulgences.

58. Once known for its site of superb scenic beauty, Jeju island now faces the risk of losing its reputation as being one of the World Heritage Sites. The increasing level of logging, sudden expansion of human settlement, and the loss of historical authenticity of these heritage values have led to disappointment among those who have advocated its scenic beauty. Insufficient management systems contributed to the increase of pollution which was triggered by the use of advanced technologies such as cars and high-tech machinery. The revitalizing mood once present in Jeju's environment is _____.

(a) the most interesting aspect of visiting the Jeju island

(b) a pleasant memory that resides only in the past

(c) a sign of human activity that destroys nature.

(d) an indication of what would happen to other cultural heritages.

59. Many East Asian countries including China or Japan have a large portion of their population engaging in the field of aquaculture, which is any activity related to the farming or cultivating of aquatic organisms. Currently, this industry is on a downfall due to the sudden decrease in the number of wild fisheries in the neighboring seas since the end of the 1990s. This complication has even worsened with the consequent fall of various international organizations which have experience in purifying ocean water. In the East-Asian region, it can be clearly observed that the aquaculture business _____.

(a) remains an ongoing success that allows for future development

(b) is no longer beneficial but rather a loss

(c) has continuously reduced in profit

(d) is left as an industry that our future generation must focus on

60. Many Cherokee tribes living in the Smoky Mountains located in Tennessee have _____, but not so much anymore. The fundamental reason for this comes from the sudden drop in the population of the tribal members in the local area. This has thus led to the lack of people capable of captivating such beasts in the mountain region. With this drastic change, a large majority of the Cherokee's eating habits have leaned excessively towards fruits or vegetables, as it requires less labor to obtain.

(a) had a diet mainly consisted of large animals

(b) had vegetarian ways of living

(c) been regarded as violent and brutal

(d) become sick from an unknown disease

주제 찾기

1. Dear Ms. Lee

   The University of Amsterdam is excited to have you as an exchange student. We would like to inform you that your arrangement at the SK Global Dormitory has been arranged and a local student has been selected to be your roommate to help you adjust to your one semester in Amsterdam. However, we do need your confirmation that your decision to come to the University of Amsterdam is finalized. Please sign and fill out the form attached to this email and send it back to us via fax.

   Q: What is the main purpose of the letter?

   (a) To congratulate the applicant on her acceptance

   (b) To ask for a final confirmation to be sent

   (c) To inform the applicant of the details of her visit to Amsterdam

   (d) To introduce a roommate

2. Dear Mr. Rauguin

   We have received your request to permanently delete your Faccialibro account. We must inform you, however, that the terms and conditions that you willingly agreed to during your registration process states that Faccialibro has no duty to remove your personal data upon the deletion of your account, and we will continue to use them for selective advertisement.
   Although we provide no means to remove your data, a cancellation fee of 5,000 USD will let you receive no further advertisements from our service. Please inform us of your intentions regarding this matter.
   Sincerely, Marco Giucoberco

   Q: What is the main purpose of the letter to Mr. Rauguin?

   (a) To inform him that he needs to register for an account

   (b) To discuss the matter concerning the deletion of his account

   (c) To ask that he pay the 5,000USD of cancellation fee as soon as possible

   (d) To enquire whether or not he wishes to remove his Faccialibro account

3. For two weeks, 20 men and women competed in the wilderness of Amazon all day and all night, desperately fighting for survival. They are competing against each other for the final grand prize of $5,000,000 and an offer to be the next Man vs Wild cameraman. Some of the competitors who were hardy and fit had much bad luck during the game. Meanwhile, there were others who seemed too frail and unfit for the wild but overcame their weaknesses with luck or wit. All of them, however, share the same dream of becoming a millionaire and going back to America.

Q: What is the main topic of the passage?

(a) The goal of competitors fighting for survival

(b) The competition for the grand prize on a TV survival show

(c) The requirements to become the next Man vs Wild cameraman

(d) The winners of the grand prize in the TV show Survival Amazon

4. Fresh Me has officially launched a new dental line, Fresh Teeth. Fresh Teeth is a non-chemical mixture of mint and eucalyptus extracts that removes stains, plaques, and even bad breathe. Apply Fresh Teeth twice a day instead of regular toothpaste, and you will definitely witness a dramatic change within a month. You will experience a plaque reduction of up to 65 percent and a dramatic whitening effect of 36 percent. This amazing offer is now available only at $20 with additional discount available with the purchase of two!

Q: What is mainly being advertised in the passage?

(a) A toothpaste that is very effective

(b) A 65% discount on toothpaste

(c) A way to reduce bad breathe

(d) A plaque-free toothpaste

5. Making a piñata is not as difficult as people might think. First, make paper mache paste by mixing a bowl of flour with water. Second, tear some newspapers into strips. They should be about 2 inches wide and 6 to 8 inches long; making the newspaper to lie nice and flat on the balloon. Next, apply paper mache in a crisscross pattern until the entire balloon is covered. Let the piñata sit until it is completely dried and hardened. After that, pop the balloon and remove it, leaving the mold empty in a balloon-shaped.

Q: What is the passage mainly about?

(a) How to make a sphere-shaped mold

(b) Being careful with handling a balloon

(c) Solution to difficulties of making a piñata with paper mache

(d) Steps necessary for constructing a piñata

6. Until the late 19th century, women's garment had the silhouette of an hourglass. Blouses and dresses were full in front and a narrow waist supported by a corset was highlighted with a sash or a belt. However, the silhouette slimmed down and elongated dramatically as the new century began. Dresses became much more fluid and soft than before. In later years, women's fashion tilted towards accessibility and practicality as women entered the workforce and earned rights to vote. The constrictive corset, an imperative part of women's garments in highlighting a thin waist, became a thing of the past.

Q: What is the passage mainly about?

(a) Late 19th century fashion movement

(b) The history of women's garment in the transition of the century

(c) How dress designs changed over time

(d) Transformation in women's trend

7. Police authorities have developed a new method that is effective in distinguishing fake identifications. Minors illegally forge a bogus ID mainly in order to get into bars and to purchase alcohol or cigarettes. These IDs seem legitimate to a naked eye, making it even harder for bar owners to spot. The government has come up with an authorized system, which recognizes the barcode on the back of an ID card, showing not only the general information and records but also a fingerprint for comparison. With the new technology, authorities are hoping to prevent the usage of fake IDs.

Q: What is the passage mainly about?

(a) How effectively the new system catches phony IDs

(b) The police authorities' efforts to arrest minors using forged IDs

(c) A fingerprint system that works well

(d) The introduction of a new system for catching fake identifications

8. Born in New York in 1915, the mathematician Jeremy Macbeth originally studied English literature at Harvard. Afterwards, he served in the US Army during the Second World War. As a lieutenant in the army signal corps, he gained experience in encrypting and decrypting transmissions. That was when he realized his talent in math. When the war ended, he went on to study math and cryptology. Professor Macbeth's prolific research in the field is very widely known today.

Q: What is the best title for the passage?

(a) Jeremy Macbeth's Military Service during World War II

(b) Jeremy Macbeth: How a Shakespearean turned into a mathematician

(c) Jeremy Macbeth's Unexpected Talent in Cryptology and Mathematics

(d) Jeremy Macbeth's Treason against Literature for Mathematics and Cryptology

9. When Guiltius II became the pope, he used art as an educational tool to propagate the divine wisdom even to the ignorant. He instructed the best craftsmen of the time to create sculptures and murals form the Bible. Thus were created the magnificent paintings in the Notre Dame de Montie-Python, and the masterful sculptures in the Baptistery of Saint Claus, both depicting the life and death of Christ. Such religious artworks acted as a method of teaching stories in the Bible even to the illiterate.

Q: What is the passage mainly about?

(a) Pope Guiltius II's use of artworks for religious purposes

(b) Pope Guiltius II's strong belief in educating the ignorant

(c) Pope Guiltius II's relations with religious medieval craftsmen

(d) Popo Guiltius II's achievements in the field of paintings and sculpture

10. The asteroid B-613 has a surface made up of highly rare elements, since it is constantly being bombarded with extreme cosmic radiation. An anomalous supernova nearby is spraying the asteroid with a powerful ray of energy, continuously converting rocks to uncommon matter. These elements usually have an extremely short half-life, and disappear immediately after they are created. On B-613, however, the rare elements are constantly fed energy, making it possible to sustain its unstable form. As a result, B-613 is the only known place in the universe where Doloresumbridsium and Albusdumbledorium can be found.

Q: What is the main topic of the passage?

(a) Elements on the surface of B-613

(b) The creation of rare elements in B-613

(c) The powerful radiation of an anomalous supernova

(d) The forces behind the unusual stabilization of rare elements

11. One of Percival Anthony's bestselling novels, Helen's Mistress, was released in 1926 and instantly became the bestseller across the United States. In many ways, it is a reflection of the author's trauma, an epitaph that commemorated an innocence lost. Together with the pessimistic atmosphere of the time during the Great Depression, its stark portrayal of a dreadful and morbid childhood attracted many sympathetic readers.

Q: What is the main topic of the passage?

(a) The socio-historical context of the success of Helen's Mistress

(b) The factors that contributed to the release of Helen's Mistress

(c) The overall atmosphere of the United States in the 1920s

(d) The common theme of Percival Tumbledoor's novels

12. The 1938 fluoric acid containment breach wiped off 30 different species of plants and animals in the town of San Bronzino, providing the first actual evidence that fluoric acid leakage can cause devastating damage to the regional flora and fauna. "It was a disaster", one witness of the incident said. "The green fields suddenly turned into a lifeless wasteland". Our investigation conducted in the area revealed that the area is still heavily contaminated after nearly a century since the incident, leading to pessimistic predictions on whether the region will ever be able to recover.

Q: What is the best title for the passage?

(a) An Investigation into Catastrophic Chemical Breach in San Bronzino

(b) Preventing Ecological Damage due to Fluoric Acid Containment Breach

(c) The Oldest Evidence of Chemical Breach Causing Ecological Damage

(d) A Drop in Regional Species Count due to Fluoric Acid Breach

13. Holi, also known as the Festival of Colors, is the Hindu religious festival that is widely known for the use of colored powders. Colored powders being thrown at each other represents the celebration of spring and a new beginning. Contrary to recent reports on the usage of chemically produced industrial dyes, people still extract natural pigments from flowers and leaves for the coloration of powder. Due to its religious background, people preserve the old tradition of applying turmeric, sandalwood paste, or extracts of plants. Following the custom of utilizing natural resources adds another reason to why Holi is a sacred religious ritual as well as a festival with joy and excitement

Q: What is the main point of the advertisement?

(a) Holi is celebrated at the start of the new season

(b) Natural colors have been continuously used since the past

(c) Colored powders were labeled as synthetic due to environmental reasons

(d) Flowers and leaves contain color pigments

14. With the advent of New Year, people are determined to follow their New Year's resolutions. From losing twenty pounds to learning a foreign language, various goals are set with a sense of hope and motivation. The plan is somewhat unrealistic, however, if the goal is too broad or not organized in a detailed manner. In epitome, "losing weight" sounds way too vague to achieve, in which a person might be overwhelmed even before the start. To prevent such happenings, one should come up with concrete ideas to materialize the plan. "Going to the gym at 7 A.M." or "eating more vegetables instead of junk foods" is more realistic. It is indeed always better to have details in actualizing the goal.

Q: What is the writer's main advice for achieving a goal?

(a) The importance of objective cannot be highlighted more

(b) Specific details impede an individual's success

(c) Be strict to oneself in keeping personal promises

(d) Detailed plans are necessary to accomplish goals

15. Individuals, schools, and societies are gearing toward practicality over true interests or talents. Due to financial reasons in relations to one's future job opportunities, career and income, people choose fields of study that can lead to a "decent, high-paying job". As a result, the studies of engineering, business administration, and medicine are preferred to the fundamental studies of physics, linguistics, and history. The perpetuation of the trend will weaken the cornerstone of all studies and even the research and development of various sectors. Thus, the society will become imbalanced, and ultimately its overall growth and advancement are hindered.

Q: What is the main idea of the passage?

(a) Academic institutions should provide more support for opportunities of advancement

(b) Detrimental societal impacts are expected due to extensive curricular of fundamental studies

(c) The tendency to focus on practicality will result in negative repercussions

(d) Studies that can be easily applied in the real work environment should be emphasized over those that cannot be applied

16. Consumption of animal flesh has been a part of human diet from the dawn of humanity. Consequently, it has become a significant aspect in the establishments of cultures and languages. Religious practices have long since been associated with the consumption of meat, like the Abrahmic tradition of butchering animals in the Halal or Kosher method. The etymology of various types of meat is also entangled with our history. The English words representing the meat of cows, pigs and sheep all correspond to the French terms for the animals themselves, like beef from the French boeuf, pork from porc, and mutton as in mouton.

Q: What is the main topic of the passage?

(a) The influence of meat in human culture

(b) The consumption of meat from early history

(c) The words associated with meat in English

(d) The necessity of protein from animal flesh consumption

17. It is a well-known fact that Tasty Mango Islands will face a drastic increase in their population over the next century or so. However, as UNICEF official Abdul Hassukh pointed out, that is not a fact that we can be optimistic about. The lack of land and social infrastructure in the islands will make the country face a grave challenge handling the increase in population. By 2050, the population of Tasty Mango Island is expected to reach 10 million. In the small landmass of the islands, there would only be 1.44 square meters of space per person. That means the island will literally be full of people, unless the government reacts with appropriate policies to counter the problem.

Q: What is the best title for the passage?
(a) Tasty Mango Islands, the Land of Tranquility
(b) Immigration Problem; What is the government doing?
(c) UNICEF Official Warns of an impending global crisis
(d) Rising Population Causes Concern of Overpopulation

18. Poaching can be an exciting and rewarding career. And there are all kinds of places to go poaching out there, away from the eyes of law. Poachers need to have sharp instincts to find wild animals and approach them without being detected, and also know when the police are coming for you. Do you have what it takes to become a poacher? Are you ready to live the romantic life roaming the African plains? Then, the Latchford Poaching Coaching will provide you with the training to become a professional poacher. Suitable applicants will join us for our trip to Serengeti late this year. Contact us now at 1544-7979 for more information.

Q: What is the main idea of the advertisement?
(a) Latchford Poaching Coaching offers a trip to Serengeti
(b) Poaching is a very dangerous occupation, which entails many difficult tasks
(c) Latchford Poaching Coaching is looking for suitable individuals to train as poachers
(d) Poaching positions open at Latchford Poaching

19. Dear Mrs. Thompson,

With accordance to the Calculus class rules, I left my last Calculus exam paper on your desk for a correction. The syllabus said to leave the test in your office for any questions or mistakes. I have not altered any answers and it is in the same state as you handed out yesterday.

My answer for question number 9 seems to pass as an alternative solution according to what the textbook elaborates on the equation. It seems that other students got partial credit for the alternative answer in which, for some reason, I was not able to receive. I would appreciate it if you would take a look at the problem and let me know if I could receive the credit.

Sincerely,

Tim Jackson

Q: What is the email mainly about?

(a) A request for full credit on the question

(b) A mistake made on question number 9

(c) An appeal for a re-scoring of the calculus exam

(d) A calculus test having intricate equations

20. Renowned psychologists and linguists have continuously researched the correlation of the human mind and language. Widely known as "The Power of Words," scientists have been proving how a simple change of words could lead to tremendous or unexpected transitions. In epitome, people simply ignored and passed by a blind man holding a sign of "Changes Appreciated" on the subway. However, as the blind man held up a new sign that says, "It is a beautiful day, but I cannot see it", people were moved by the inspiring phrase, donating their change and even large amounts of money to help the blind man.

Q: What is the passage mainly about?

(a) How the relationship between language and human psychology has led to a mishap

(b) The experiment done to a blind man on the subway

(c) The profound influence of donation on a person

(d) The display of Power of Words and its effect

21. Library and Information Science (LIS) is the combination of two fields of studies: library science and information science. It has first started as a professional training program then developed into a university-level academic institution amid the mid-20th century. Information, especially nowadays, is a crucial asset. Thus, the education of LIS cannot be highlighted any further. However, many scholars question the core concept of the field, some emphasizing computing and internetworking concepts and skills while others claiming that LIS is a social science reguiring a mix of practical skills in ethnography and interviewing. The domain still seems open to debate.

Q: What is the best title for the passage?

(a) The importance of educating students with computing skills

(b) How interviewing affects the study of LIS

(c) The questionable nature of the LIS field

(d) The rise of information in the mid-20th century

22. Mitochondrion is undoubtedly the energy factory of all cells, including for both animal and plant cells. It has a tremendous influence on the cell growth and the control of the cell cycle. The process of respiration, using the oxygen to generate energy, produces adenosine triphosphate (ATP), a key element of the mitochondrion. Then, ATP is used as the source of chemical energy in which it enables the mitochondria to supply important cellular energy. Mitochondrion is also involved in other cellular activities, such as cellular differentiation, signaling, and cell death.

Q: What does mitochondrion mainly do?

(a) It helps ATP to produce oxygen

(b) It produces ATP, which is where energy comes from

(c) It has a tremendous influence on the birth and death of a cell

(d) It controls the cell cycle

23. Would you like to save a bundle on computers? Build one yourself instead of buying the more expensive brand-manufactured ones. A price comparison between finished product computers and the sum of its parts showed that building a computer yourself can save up to 40% of your budget. A research that took place for over three years in local computer rental shops also proved that brand-name computers require maintenance costs at only 5 dollars less per year. That's not that much, and considering how quickly people buy new computers these days, building a computer yourself is a much better bargain.

Q: What is the main idea of the passage?

(a) Research on computer maintenance cost was performed at PC cafes

(b) Manufactured computers tend to last longer than built-at-home computers

(c) Considering various factors, it is more economical to build a computer than to buy one

(d) A research has proven that computers built at home incur less maintenance cost over time

24. If you are looking for mental training that will bring your spirit closer to the realm of Ahnas-hol, there is a place just for you. Our training center La Merde qui Danse provides training activities that will cleanse your body and mind. We offer, just for $59.99 per month, a diverse range of training regimen to release mind-toxins from your body and capture Ahnas, the essence of our soul. The following are only a part of what we have to offer: a bone-breaker yoga session, a geomagnetic levitation training and a defense against the dark arts class.
In case you happen to doubt the truth of our claims, we give you an unbelievable 30 day money-back guarantee. Make your call now.

Q: What is the advertisement mainly about?

(a) What it takes you to become Ahnas-hol

(b) A range of activities offered to help with mental training

(c) An offer for an unbelievable 30 day money-back guarantee

(d) A training to capture mind-toxins and retain them in the body

25. Despite safety measures, Pneumotraumatic Fibrosis is a prevalent condition amongst our factory personnel, affecting nearly 56% of all full-time workers. The employee policy at Newt & Claire Co. entitles all personnel suffering from the disorder to employee welfare benefits. Around 50% of the employees are currently beneficiaries of this policy, and this is causing quite a burden on our company welfare budget. Although the exact number is uncertain, the benefit costs the company approximately 500,000 dollars each year. This is outrageous, and must be brought to attention immediately.

Q: What is the passage mainly about?

(a) Health problems prevalent among Newt & Claire workers

(b) The symptoms of pneumotraumatic fibrosis on Newt & Claire workers

(c) The heavy burden of employee healthcare on the company welfare budget

(d) A plan to build another welfare center for the company board of directors in Newt & Claire

26. The Sinocentric ideal of Joseon had been widespread when the country was merely a couple of hundred years old. But by the end of the Japanese Invasion in 1600 CE, the Ming dynasty began to sway and give way to the newly-risen Qing dynasty. The Qing dynasty was founded by the Manchu people, who most Koreans considered barbarians. Shortly after, when the Qing dynasty started demanding recognition and assumed the leading role in the Sinocentric Asian politics, the people of Joseon became reluctant and furious, ultimately providing the cause of two subsequent wars between the nations.

Q: What is the main topic of the passage?

(a) Joseon's transformation to an independent nation

(b) The fall of the Ming dynasty after the Japanese invasion of Korea

(c) The process leading up to the conflict between Joseon and the Qing dynasty

(d) The Qing dynasty's invasion due to Joseon's hostility in the 17th century Asia

정답표

정답표

교재1~19단원	예제	Q2	Q3	Q4	Q5
1	—	—	—	—	—
2	B	C	C	B	D
3	D	A	B	A	A
4	B	A	D	A	C
5	D	C	C	C	A
6	B	B	A	C	D
7	B	A	D	C	C
8	D	B	C	C	B
9	A	B	A	D	C
10	B	C	A	D	B
11	D	C	C	C	B
12	D	C	A	D	C
13	B	A	D	C	D
14	A	A	C	C	B
15	A	C	A	B	D
16	C	D	B	D	A
17	D	A, D (복수정답)	A	B	D
18	C	D	D	A	C
19	—	—	—	—	—

기존 문제 리뷰 및 총정리 – 빈칸채우기

1	2	3	4	5	6	7	8	9	10
A	D	C	A	C	D	A	A	B	B

11	12	13	14	15	16	17	18	19	20
C	A	B	C	C	B	A	C	D	B

21	22	23	24	25	26	27	28	29	30
C	A	D	B	A	B	A	A	D	B

31	32	33	34	35	36	37	38	39	40
A	D	D	C	A	C	C	A	B	B

41	42	43	44	45	46	47	48		
A	A	A	C	D	A	A	C		

기존 문제 리뷰 및 총정리 - 주제찾기

1	2	3	4	5	6	7	8	9	10
D	D	D	C	C	B	C	C	D	A
11	12	13	14	15	16	17	18	19	20
D	C	C	B	C	D	C	B	D	C
21									
B									

쏘아보기 적용 실전문제 - 빈칸채우기

1	2	3	4	5	6	7	8	9	10
A	A	B	C	B	A	B	B	C	D
11	12	13	14	15	16	17	18	19	20
C	A	B	A	A	C	B	D	D	B
21	22	23	24	25	26	27	28	29	30
D	A	B	A	C	B	C	A	A	D
31	32	33	34	35	36	37	38	39	40
D	C	D	B	A	C	C	D	A	A
41	42	43	44	45	46	47	48	49	50
C	A	A	D	D	D	D	D	C	D
51	52	53	54	55	56	57	58	59	60
C	D	B	D	D	C	D	B	C	A

쏘아보기 적용 실전문제 - 주제찾기

1	2	3	4	5	6	7	8	9	10
B	B	A	A	D	B	D	C	A	D
11	12	13	14	15	16	17	18	19	20
A	A	B	D	C	A	D	C	C	D
21	22	23	24	25	26				
C	C	C	B	C	C				

☞ 2주차 수업이 마치고 그 사이에 정기시험이 하나 있었는데, 2주사이에 배웠던 기술들만 보고도 엄청 많이
도움이 됐어요. 그리고 결국 8회 수업을 완강했습니다. 2달동안 배운게 체화되기 까지 젤 노력을 많이 한것 같아요.
쌤께서 수강후에도 지속적으로 지도해주셔서 깜짝놀랐어요.
덕분에 시험전날 까지 내 약점을 보완하는 학습법을 유지할 수 있었고, 결국 목표점수800보다 훨씬 높은 849점
달성했습니다!!!

☞ 텝스가 발목을 잡던 저에겐 최고의 수업이었습니다. 이런 내용을 제공해주신 선생님께 진심으로 감사드리는 바입니다.
의전원 합격했습니다. 제 인생을 바꿔주신 은인이네요. 감사드립니다.

☞ 제가 예전에 최고 점수가 500점대 후반이었습니다. 제 목표는 700점, 첫 시간에 작성하는 설문지에도 목표점수를
700점으로 적어냈습니다. 첫 수업부터 깜짝놀랐고, 지금 까지 내가 공부해온 방법이 잘못됐구나…… 라는 것을
느꼈습니다. 첫 수업 이후로는 쌤께서 시키시는 대로 믿고 따라갔더니, 한 달 후에 시험에서 680점을 달성했습니다.
그 이후로는 선생님께서 제시해주시는 문제풀이법에 대한 강한 확신이 생겼고 무조건 교재만 따라서 공부했습니다.
그러니까 다음시험에서 770점이 나왔습니다. 8번의 수업으로 이렇게 점수가 변할 수 있다는게 신기합니다.
텝스19에 등록안했으면 지금도 텝스 시험을 치고 있었겠죠??ㅎㅎㅎ 선생님 감사해요!
TEPS19 강추합니다.

☞ 저는 수업한달 듣고 60점이 상승했습니다. 지금도 수업교재를 여러번 반복하고 있는 중, 오늘 시험을 첫습니다.
평상시에는 독해시간이 항상 부족했는데, 오늘은 좀 자신있게 다 풀었습니다. 앞으로 2번 정도 텝스 시험을 더 칠려고
합니다. 정말 감사드립니다.

☞ 저는 독해문제를 평균적으로 3문제정도 마지막 일분에 급하게풀거나 찍는 그러한 패턴을 갖고있었는데 이 수업을 듣고
배운 기술들을 체화하고 나니 다풀고나서 체크해둔 문제를 한두문제정도 검토할수있는 시간이 남게되었고 그 정확도도
많이 올라가서 잘나와도 350이었던 독해점수가 384점까지 나왔습니다.
처음에 저는 배운 기술들을 참신하고 유용하다고만 생각하고 단편적으로 적용하는정도에 그치고 완전한 체화에는
게을렀습니다. 실제로 그러한 단편적 적용으로도 시간의 단축은 많이 일어났고 어느 정도 점수의 상승도 있었습니다.
그러나 정확도가 향상되지는 않았기에 한계가 느껴졌습니다. 그렇게 가벼운적용에 대한 문제의식을 느끼고나서부터
개념교재만을 여러번읽고 체화시키는데에 집중하였더니 신기할정도로 정확도가 오른것을 알게되었습니다.
그렇게 저는 최고점 899점에서 946점으로 강사분께서 말씀하신 900점과 950점의 차이가 단 하나라는 사실을
직접 경험했습니다.
강사님, 감사합니다!

☞ 3월에 독해 기술을 거의 다 배우긴 하는데 4월강의까지 듣고 나서야 완성되는 느낌이 들었습니다.
　수강 결과, 2월에 시험 848점에서 시작하여 4월 7일 시험에서 910점으로 상승했습니다. 거의 독해에서 올린 점수라
　강의 효과를 많이 봤다는 생각이 듭니다. 감사드립니다 선생님~ 저처럼 텝스 점수가 필요하지만 공부할 시간이
　부족한 분들께 텝스 19 강추드리고 싶습니당.

☞ 우선 감사의 말씀부터 드리겠습니다. 반년동안 대형어학원을 다니다가 성적이 항상 너무 불안정해서
　TEPS19에 등록하게 되었고, 결국 130점 올랐습니다. 정말 다른 접근법들과는 많이 다르다는 걸 느낍니다.
　내 실력과 점수가 오르는 것이 느껴집니다. 회사 이미지만 믿고 다니던 학원들과는 다른게 느껴집니다.
　선생님 감사드려요.

☞ 이제 짧은 2달이었지만 청해, 문법, 어휘, 독해 시험요령을 잘 이해했고, 시간날때마다 짬을 내어 꾸준히 영어공부를
　해 나갈 생각입니다. 특히 독해는 모든 영어의 기본임을 새삼 느꼈고 19가지 텝스문제풀이 기술은 문장의
　전체적인 구성과 뉘앙스, 그리고 영어의 새로운 묘미를 느끼게 해주는 것 같습니다. 그동안 수고하셨고,
　특히 지난번 구정때 참석못한 수강생을 위한 동영상강의는 감동적이었습니다. 텝스 19강의 무궁한 발전을 기원합니다.

☞ 첫 수업을 듣고서 확신이 든 것은 확실히 "시험은 시험을 보는 방법이 따로 있다"는 것입니다.
　teps19 skill을 알기 전까진 TEPS는 해외에서 살다와서 전날 대충 모의고사 한번 보구서 900점대 나오는 그런 막연하고
　불평등한 시험이라는 편견이 강했습니다. 하지만 저같은 텝스 점수 최고점이 고작 671점인 사람도 Skill을 써서
　900점대에 진입 혹은 근처에는 갈 수 있다는 확신이 섰습니다.

☞ 수업을 들으니 어떤 편법적인 요령이라기보다 논지를 전개하는 글의 특성상 필연적일 수 밖에 없는 글의 구조를 눈으로
　확인하고 나니 아, 당연하겠구나, 그렇구나 하는 감탄사가 절로 나네요. 그걸 그렇게 체계화해서 분석했다는 사실이
　놀라울 따름입니다. 직장인에, 가정주부에 공부할 시간을 좀처럼 내기 어려운 상황에서 효율적인 방법을 통해 공부하는
　데 많은 도움이 될 거 같습니다.
　믿고 따라오라는 선생님 말씀 새기겠습니다.

☞ 5월달 수업듣고 종강하고 7월달 텝스에서 140점 올랐네요 ㅜㅜ더 열심히 해서 더 많이 올려야 겠어요.
　감사합니다.

☞ 처음에는 새로운 방식에 적응도 안되고 30초 안에 문제를 풀라는 말이 불가능해보였습니다. 하지만 수업이 방법론을
　알려주는 것이다 보니 참 현실적이라는 생각이 들기 시작했습니다. 문제 풀다보면 감이 올때가 있잖아요,
　하지만 혼자 공부를 하다보면 느낌으로만 느끼고 놓쳐버릴 때가 많죠 하지만 이 수업에서는 그런 느낌을 집어서
　형식화해 전달해줍니다. 이렇게 문제풀이 방법을 배우다 보니 좀더 효과적으로 공부를 할 수 있다고 생각합니다.
　그럼 다들 열공해서 원하는 바를 성취합시다.

☞ 텝스 19 수업을 들으면서 텝스 지문을 보는 눈이 달라졌습니다. 텝스 시험 속에 녹아있는 논리와 근거를 이해하면서
　성적 상승에 대한 희망이 생겼습니다. 처음에 의구심 가득 안고 시작했던 것이 8번의 수업이 끝나면서
　선생님에 대한 무한 신뢰로 바뀌었네요. 목표 점수 달성하는 그 날까지 텝스 19 접근법 반복 또 반복하겠습니다.
　선생님 그 동안 수고 많으셨구요. 감사합니다.

☞ 제가 수능준비를 하면서 같이 어학특기자 전형으로 준비하고있는 고3인데용 정말 텝스 19가지 스킬을 배우면서 많은
   도움이 되었습니다 그리고 앞으로 성적변화도 기대가 되고요!

☞ 처음 수업듣기전에는 정말 반신반의하면서 신청했고, 첫 수업을 듣고 '정말 성적 향상이 가능할까' 라고 의심했던 것도
   사실입니다. 하지만 어제 마지막 수업을 마치고, 스스로 공부하면서 저도 모르게 독해를 바라보는 눈이 달라졌다는
   것을 느꼈습니다. 19가지의 기술을 반복하고 또 읽고 적용하고. 19가지 기술을 모두 배우고 나니깐 무엇을 먼저
   읽어야 하는지, 어떤 문장이 진짜 중요한 문장인지 그리고 선택지에 어떻게 함정을 파놓았는지까지 하나씩 눈에 보이기
   시작했습니다. 막연한 독해가 아니라 정말 텝스를 위한 독해, 아니 이게 "진짜 독해"구나 싶었습니다.

☞ 정말 텝스 점수를 단기간에 올리기 원하시는 분들에게 강추하는 강의입니다.
   중간에 다른데 찾아가지 마시고, 여기서 하라는 대로만 하시면 점수는 반드시 오르게 되어있습니다.
   모두들 파이팅!

☞ Teps19를 수강하면서 저에게 일어난 가장 큰 변화는 teps 공부의 접근 방법이었습니다. Teps19 수강 이전에는
   혼자 공부하며 무작정 문제집만 풀었습니다. 하지만 강의를 듣고보니 혼자 공부해왔던 방법이 얼마나 비효율적이었는지
   깨달았고 선생님께서 안내해 주시는 데로 따라다 보니 현재 리딩 50점 정도의 점수가 올랐습니다.
   점수도 RC뿐 아니라 LC, 어휘, 문법까지 전반적으로 상승하였네요.
   Tpes 19없이 제가 공부하던 방법으로 계속 공부하였더라면 점수는 아마 아직도 제자리 걸음이었을 것입니다.
   Teps만 집중적으로 공부하였더라면 훨씬 높은 점수를 받았을 텐데…… 그러지 못한 것이 많이 아쉽지만, 앞으로 목표
   점수에 도달할 때까지 Teps 19만 믿고 충실히 공부할 예정입니다. 2달간 좋은 강의 해주신 선생님께 감사드립니다.

☞ 2달간의 수업이 끝났습니다. 수업을 들을때 재미있게 들어서 시간가는줄 몰랐습니다. 선생님의 상세한 설명은
   많은 도움이 된 거 같습니다. 요번달에 시험을 보고 skill을 적용해보고 점수를 올려야겠습니다. 각 파트마다
   체계화된 방식으로 문제푸는 방식이 자신감을 상승시키는거 같습니다. 복습과 반복학습 적용해서 앞으로 텝스를
   정복해나가겠습니다. 선생님 수고하셨습니다.^^

☞ 유명한 학원이다, 잘하는 강사다, 꼭 풀어야 하는 문제집이다…… 열심히 챙겨서 텝스를 준비했었습니다.
   나름 노력하고 열심히 한다고 했는데…… 이놈의 텝스는 번번히 제 뒷통수를 치더군요.
   '이제 정말 마지막이다' 라는 마음으로 Teps19를 수강하게되었습니다. 그리고 수업 첫시간에 깨달았습니다.
   왜 텝스점수를 내지 못하고 있는지를……
   Teps19는 문제 지문을 보는 관점부터가 달랐습니다. 그동안 풀고 정답 찾기에 급급했던 것에서 벗어나 지문을 쏘아보니
   큰 그림이 그려지듯 보이더군요. ㅎㅎ Teps19를 수강하길 행운이었다고 생각합니다.

☞ 기존에 공부하던 방식보다 체계적이고 논리적인 방식에 매수업마다 새로 웠습니다.
   텝스 19 수업을 조금 더 일찍 들을걸 하는 아쉬움도 남지만 얼마 남지 않은 시간 동안 수업에서 배운 부분들을 체화시켜
   선생님 말씀대로 지금의 점수보다 점수를 극대화 시키도록 최선을 다해 보고자 합니다.
   감사합니다~!!

☞ 막판에 텝스19에 의지 하게 되었는데 , 그 선택이 틀리지 않았다고 생각합니다. 아직 마지막 결과는 안나왔지만 꼭 좋은 결과가 있을거 라고 감히 이렇게 전합니다. 19가지 스킬에 근거한 텝스 정복! 후회하지 않습니다.^^ 그리고 선생님 감사합니다.

☞ 진작에 이 수업을 시작했다면 지난 시간 동안 다른 학원들 다니면서 돈 쓰지 않았을텐데 ㅠㅠ 하는 생각이 듭니다. 무작정 첫문장부터 내달려왔던 습관에서 벗어난 것, 중요한 부분을 찾아읽는, 텝스 본연의 리딩에 대해 알게 되어 기쁩니다!

☞ 첫 수업을 듣고 정말 이게 될까라는 생각도 들었지만 선생님을 믿고 그 방법대로 문제를 풀었더니 정말 시간이 확 줄었고 정확도도 올라갔습니다. 솔직히 문제를 풀면서도 확신이 없었던적이 많았지만 선생님이 제시해주신 방법대로 풀면서 점점 확신이 생기기 시작했습니다. 단기간에 성적향상이 되는것도 좋지만 무엇보다 텝스에 대한 올바른 접근법을 알게되어서 나중에 혼자 텝스 공부를 할때에도 큰 도움이 될 것이라고 믿습니다.

☞ 공부를 해도 텝스점수가 안 올라서 포기해야하나 했는데 쌤 수업듣고 다시 용기내서 공부합니다. 선생님이 알려주신 기술대로라면 점수가 오를거 같아요!!! 담주 시험까지 열씨미 할께요.

☞ 이전과 다른 수업내용을 통해 자신감이 생겼다. 시간싸움인 텝스에서 독해 영역 점수가 다른 파트에 비해 많이 낮았는데, 이번 수업을 듣고, 19개의 스킬들(?)을 배우면서 독해 40문제를 풀고 시간이 남아 스스로도 놀랬다. 수업을 듣기 전 어떻게 문장 1-2개만을 가지고 문제를 접근할 수 있는가. 거짓말 같았는데 문제출제의 원리를 파악하고, 적응하고 체화해 가면서 의심이 사라졌다.

☞ 매 수업 스킬들 하나하나 배울때마다 선생님께서 그동안 얼마나 텝스 분석을 많이하셨을지 생각하게 됩니다. 그렇게 시간에 걸쳐 노력이 많이 깃든, 검증된 분석 내용을 배울 수 있다는게 행운인것 같네요, 감사드립니다!

☞ 이전에는 글을 처음부터 끝까지 한번에 빠르게 읽고 내용을 이해하려 노력했습니다. 보통 7문제에서 10문제정도 찍었습니다. 그러나 이제는 텝스 독해의 요령과 스킬들을 익히면서 속도가 많이 붙어 제 시간안에 모든 문제를 다 풀거나 한 두문제 못푸는 정도입니다. 결과적으로 점수가 많이 올랐습니다. 앞으로 좀더 숙달이 된다면 820점 이상도 가능하리라 생각됩니다.

☞ 기술하나하나 빈칸에 적용되는게 너무 신기하네요 !강의를 좀더 빨리 알았으면 어땠을까하는 생각이 자꾸듭니다.

☞ 수고가 많으십니다 선생님의 분석력에 많이 놀랐습니다 덕분에 목표 달성했습니다 감사합니다.

☞ 시간투자 대비 산출면에서 효율이 짱입니다. 점수별 분반이 필요없이 누구에게나 도움되는것 같습니다. 강의도 명쾌하시고 정말 추천합니다!!

☞ 독해 속도가 이전에 비해 비약적으로 빨려졌습니다. 감사합니다.

☞ 짧은 시간이지만 독해속도가 확실히 빨라졌어요! 특히 주제찾는거랑 빈칸 채우는 부분에서 시간단축에 아주 크게 효과를 보았습니다. 감사합니다.

☞ 확실히 강의를 듣기 전보다 오답률도 줄고 문제 푸는 시간도 빨라졌습니다. 감사합니다

☞ 저는 독해를 시간 내에 다 풀긴 하고, 빈칸채우기와 주제찾기 문제만 틀리는데요.
제 사고방식과 텝스가 맞지 않는 부분이 있어서 답이 이해가 되지 않는 경우가 종종 있었는데 수업해주신
문제풀이방식을 생각해보면 텝스에서 요구하는 답이 이런 거였구나, 라는 생각을 이제서야 합니다.
저처럼 이미 독해 문제유형이 익숙하고, 문제풀이 경험이 충분히 있지만 독해점수가 교착상태이신 분들께 자신의
문제풀이방식의 취약점을 찾아내는데 도움이 될것이라고 생각합니다.

☞ 정말 독해 가장 답답하고 암담한 부분이었는데 어느새 가장 자신있는 파트가 되었습니다.

☞ 항상 좋은 수업 잘 듣고있습니다ㅎ 매번 다른 학원에서 받았던 수업과 달라서 좋아요.
독해에 많은 도움 됐어요 많은 거 배우고 갑니다!ㅎㅎ

☞ 텝스를 2년 넘게 공부한 사람으로써 나의 한계가 여기까지인가 좌절한 적이 많았습니다. 우연찮게 전단지를 보고
꽂혀서 바로 수업 등록을 하게 되었는데 새로운 세상을 보는 듯 하였습니다. 텝스에 자신감이 생겨났고 선생님께서
가르쳐주신 기술들이 문제들에 적용되는 것이 너무 신기하고 놀라웠습니다. 수업 너무 감사히 들었습니다.
다른 수강생들도 꼭 원하는 점수 받으셔서 이루고자 하는 목표 모두들 이루시길 바랍니다.^^

☞ 진짜 믿고 따라가시면 점수 오릅니다. 독해도 그렇지만 저는 사실 청해에서의 깨알같은 팁들이 점수 향상에 결과적으로
도움이 더 많이 되었습니다. 중위권 점수가 급하게 치고나가야 할 때 좋은 강의인 것 같습니다.
ㅠㅠ 마지막으로 쌤 고마워요 다음달에 상담받으러 갈게요.

☞ 막막하던 텝스 고득점의 길이 먼 나라의 이야기가 아니라 내 앞에 현실로 나타날 것 같은 이 기분좋은 느낌은
텝스19가 아니었다면 느끼기 힘들었을 것입니다. 특히, 독해에서의 시간 단축과 각 문제들에 대한 독창적인 접근 방식이
텝스 19에서 말하는 "속도와 정확성"이라는 두 마리 토끼를 다 잡아줄 것 같습니다.

☞ 이번 시험을 치면서 느낀것인데 내가 독해를 풀고 있구나 라는 생각이 들었습니다. 즉 제대로 풀고 있다는 생각이
들었습니다. 물로 2문제 정도 찍다시피 했지만 5주 수업듣고도 많은 발전이 있었습니다. 좋은 수업 감사합니다.